Master Your Emotions

The Ultimate Guide to Manage Your Feelings and Improving Your Self-Esteem. How to Overcome Negativity, Defeat Anxiety and Control Anger

© **Copyright 2019 by Michael Godsey- All rights reserved.**

The content contained within this book may not be reproduced, duplicated or transmitted without direct written permission from the author or the publisher.

Under no circumstances will any blame or legal responsibility be held against the publisher, or author, for any damages, reparation, or monetary loss due to the information contained within this book. Either directly or indirectly.

Legal Notice:

This book is copyright protected. This book is only for personal use. You cannot amend, distribute, sell, use, quote or paraphrase any part, or the content within this book, without the consent of the author or publisher.

Disclaimer Notice:

Please note the information contained within this document is for educational and entertainment purposes only. All effort has been executed to present accurate, up to date, and reliable, complete information. No warranties of any kind are declared or implied. Readers acknowledge that the author is not engaging in the rendering of legal, financial, medical or professional advice. The content within this book has been derived from various sources. Please consult a licensed professional before attempting any techniques outlined in this book.

By reading this document, the reader agrees that under no circumstances is the author responsible for any losses, direct or indirect, which are incurred as a result of the use of information contained within this document, including, but not limited to, — errors, omissions, or inaccuracies.

Table of Contents

Introduction 7

Chapter 1: Advantages of Mastering Your Emotions 9

    Greater Kindness in Everyday Life 9

    Higher Employee Morale and Reduced Attrition 10

    Increased Productivity 12

    Awesome Communication Skills 14

    Dealing with Challenges...14

    Reduced Chances of Addiction and Emotional Disorders.............15

    Better Leadership Skills 16

Chapter 2: How to Bring About a Shift in Emotions 19

    Utilize Information About Emotions Effectively 20

    Take Responsibility for Your Emotions and Actions 21

    Focus on Building a Higher Emotional Quotient 23

    Build Flexibility...24

    Practice Assertiveness..25

    Stay Emotionally Honest 26

    Practice Greater Empathy..27

    Cognitive Behavioral Therapy to The Rescue 29

    Avoid Labeling Feelings and Emotions 29

    Identify Recurring Patterns 30

    Respond Instead of Reacting..32

Mindfulness and Deep Breathing Help 33

Emotional Intelligence Can be Constantly Developed 34

Recognize Emotions Based on Physiological Signals 36

Tune in to Your Behavior 37

Dive into Your Subconscious Mind 38

Utilize the Mental Pause Button 39

Reduce Negative Personalization 40

Tune in to Verbal Clues 40

Handle Differences Like A Pro 41

Be an Active Listener 42

Decode Body Language 43

Psychometric tests and feedback 44

Practice Greater Light Heartedness 45

Be Open to Constructive Feedback and Criticism 46

Avoid Complaining 48

Stay Positive 49

Utilize Third Person Voice 50

Chapter 3: Managing Impulses and Delaying Gratification .. 53

Chapter 4: Overcoming Negative Emotions 59

Chapter 5: Building Self-Esteem 81

Increasing Self-esteem Through Writing and Journaling 98

Increasing Self-Esteem with Visualization 105

    Grow a Like-Minded Network or Community 110

    Participate Actively in a Cause You Strongly Believe In 110

Build Self-Esteem with Your Passion and Productivity 111

Test Yourself 111

Follow Tiny Pursuits 112

Realign Your Notion of Failure 113

Uncertainties and Risks Help You Grow 114

Develop Higher Self-Awareness 114

Habits That Destroy Your Self-Esteem, Emotions, and Positivity 115

Chapter 6: Emotions and Our Immediate Environment – Clear the Clutter 123

Releases the Feeling of Being Emotionally Stagnant 123

Creativity Thrives in a Clutter-Free Atmosphere 124

Your Immediate Environment is a Direct Reflection of Your Inner State 125

Opportunities Open Up 125

Higher Mental Focus 126

Reduces Anxiety 126

Start Small 127

Increase Productivity 127

Allow the New to Come In 128

Chapter 7: Explore Your Spiritual Side for Managing Anger and Other Destructive Emotions 129

Interpreting Dreams 131

Identify Your Positive Space 133

Meditate 134

Exercise 136

Deepen Awareness 137

Allow Intuition to Lead You 138

Make Gratitude a Habit 138

Prayers 139

Conclusion **141**

Introduction

You've heard the whole world and their grandmother talk about how important it is to control your emotions. Chances are every self-help book you pick up has something about controlling your emotions, getting a grip on how you feel and believing in yourself.

What exactly does mastering your emotions mean? How does it empower you? How does increasing your self-esteem help you in your daily life? How does managing your emotions and enhancing your self-esteem lower anxiety, anger, and other negative emotions?

Well, much more than this. Mastering your emotions is a powerful concept that goes beyond pampering yourself and indulging yourself. Building a high sense of self-esteem and self-worth is also starkly distanced from being self-centered. While self-centeredness is an unhealthy obsession with yourself, loving yourself is accepting yourself unconditionally, with all your strengths and weaknesses. And when we are able to accept ourselves unconditionally, we gain better control of our emotions and have more positivity.

Increasing your self-esteem and gaining control over your emotions is about never having to explain your weaknesses, having a profound sense of kindness for oneself, setting clear goals, and living a more fulfilled life. This only happens when we are able to rise above others' opinions about us and accept ourselves for the person we are. Mastering emotions isn't just a hollow, mushy and feel-good psychological concept; it is a real plan of action that can change your life forever.

This book presents highly valuable and researched strategies that help you embark on a rewarding journey to gain greater control of your emotions. You will learn to accept your mistakes, rise above temporary setbacks and get rid of feelings that hold you back from building a high sense of self-worth, positive interactions or leading a more fulfilled life.

There are lots of easy to follow and practical pointers to manage your emotions more effectively and help you build a high sense of self-worth that can be practiced on a daily basis to transform your life, irrespective of where you are currently at when it comes to gaining control of your emotions.

Chapter 1:
Advantages of Mastering Your Emotions

If someone asked me to choose the single largest factor that contributes to a person's success in today's complicated and volatile world, I'd say emotional intelligence or the ability to control one's emotions without batting an eyelid.

Emotional Intelligence is our ability to manage ours and others' emotions by discriminating among these feelings and using the information to guide our words, thoughts, and actions. To cut a long story short, emotional intelligence is an aggregation of your mental and emotional skills. Emotionally intelligent people enjoy a multitude of benefits in all spheres of life, including relationships, career, and social life.

Here are some ways your life can be impacted or benefited if you consciously focus on developing high emotional intelligence.

Greater Kindness in Everyday Life

One of the best benefits of high emotional intelligence is your ability to demonstrate more compassion for others both in your personal and professional sphere. This compassion allows you to connect with people at much deeper levels so you can forge meaningful relationships. Compassion can be manifested in several ways, including helping someone dealing with a personal issue by taking on their responsibilities or making small everyday decisions for the comfort/convenience of your employees.

Compassion helps you meaningfully connect with people both in your personal and professional life. You are able to reach out to people efficiently; forge more mutually fulfilling relationships and create an atmosphere of harmony and productivity. Emotional intelligence awards you greater compassion in dealing with people in various personal, professional and social scenarios.

Higher Employee Morale and Reduced Attrition

Morale may be an intangible concept in the corporate world, but its effects are highly measurable. You may not realize the value of high morale when it's there, but you will definitely know when it's missing. Think about the lateness, early departures, attrition, and sick leaves your company suffers from. When leaders take the time to build emotional intelligence and connect with their team members, it reflects in employee's morale.

Emotionally intelligent leaders who build stronger emotional ties with subordinate's witness improvement in the team's morale, lower measurable absenteeism, a higher team spirit and a greater desire to contribute to an organization's success. The emotional intelligence skill building cost can be minimal. However, the return on investment can be extremely high.

Let's get real here and call a spade a spade. Employees do not really quit roles, they quit senior managers. It is about escaping people and not positions. Emotionally intelligent leaders, who recognize emotional triggers, quickly pick up emotional clues of their team members and "customize" their approach to each member's unique emotional make-up and motivation will experience greater success in retaining employees. This should not be mistaken with not doing justice to one's own voice or feelings. It simply means presenting an accurate emotional response towards each team member to treat them with greater compassion, respect, and empathy.

The problem with most managers who do not understand the concept of emotional intelligence is they use a one size fits all approach for dealing with all employees, without understanding the emotional framework, motivators, and goals of individual team members. This one size fits all approach does not produce flattering results because personalities vary. Some people are more intrinsically motivated, while others thrive on extrinsic motivation. Some folks are quick to reveal their emotions; others aren't very comfortable sharing their feelings. Once you understand the emotional make-up of people, it becomes easy to deal with them more efficiently.

Increased Productivity

Emotional intelligence has a high correlation with an individual's work performance. Research has revealed that emotional intelligence is twice as crucial as technical/cognitive abilities even among professions such as engineering. Emotionally intelligent managers, supervisors, and leaders are way more effective in managing teams, motivating people and negotiating.

They create a more positive atmosphere with happier workers who are an asset to any organization. Happier workers translate into higher morale, low absenteeism, reduced attrition rate, and higher productivity. This leads to happier customers, more sales and higher profits.

Thus, emotional intelligence is an invaluable trait when it comes to success in the workplace. Whilst everyone within an organization possesses more or less the same technical competency and educational qualifications, only a few rise up the corporate ladder because of their ability to manage people and their emotions.

An emotionally intelligent leader who understands the true value of identifying and managing emotions can empower his/her subordinates with these skills on a daily basis. Discipline or self-regulation is essential when it comes to keeping your emotions in check, avoiding panic, remaining calm and being an asset to the team.

Emotionally intelligent folks have little trouble recognizing and managing potentially destructive emotions that can create stress and lower productivity. The approach is calmer, more confident and efficient. Rather than experiencing a touchier view, these folks depend on their ability to possess a more realistic view of themselves and others.

Awesome Communication Skills

People with well-developed emotional quotient are more efficient when it comes to expressing themselves. They possess the ability to listen attentively to other people's verbal clues, while also being able to tune into their nonverbal communication. They know exactly what to say to channelize people's strengths. They use the right words and nonverbal signals to help people feel at ease. There is little scope for misunderstanding whilst communicating with a person who has high emotional intelligence.

Emotionally intelligent people are well aware of the most compelling emotional triggers of the people around them. They know exactly how to inspire people to act. People who are able to communicate by emotionally connecting with someone are far more effective than technically competent folks who fail to demonstrate empathy while communicating with people. Emotional intelligence awards you better response skills.

Dealing with Challenges

Don't you sometimes look at some people and wonder how they are able to stay afloat through the most challenging situations and emerge even more successful than before? Chances are, these guys score high in emotional intelligence. Emotionally intelligent folks have the ability to calm their body and mind to view things from a clearer and more objective perspective. Their acts are more mindful and less panic stricken. Greater calmness, objectivity and clarity award you more resilience where life's challenges are concerned. Think about the Kungfu fighter who can take on the most powerful opponents by constantly working on martial arts skills. Emotional intelligence equips you with those skills to take on the toughest challenges life throws at you with resilience.

Reduced Chances of Addiction and Emotional Disorders

Addictions are generally a direct result of our inability to cope with emotions. People who struggle to come to terms with their emotions use addiction as a mechanism to avoid the more underlying and deeper prevailing issues. When you fail to recognize and manage negative emotions, there develops an unfortunate pattern of dependency on external factors such as food, nicotine, illegal substances, alcohol, porn and the like.

Addiction is just a means to escape from emotions you aren't willing to deal with.

Emotionally intelligent folks are lesser prone to addiction because of their awareness of their emotions and their ability to manage these emotions. They have a solid understanding of their feelings and do not struggle to deal with it. Since emotional intelligence makes you happier, more confident and balanced, there is a lesser propensity for dependence on destructive coping mechanisms.

They adapt more easily to challenges and changing scenarios in life. Emotionally intelligent people are competent in resolving differences and coming up with more positive solutions. Since they display such a high understanding of their own and others' emotions, it becomes easier for them to deal with conflicts.

Emotionally healthy people are less prone to be victims of drug abuse or binge eating disorders, which predominantly originate from much deeper psychological issues.

Better Leadership Skills

Emotionally intelligent folks possess a highly evolved ability in recognizing and understanding factors that drive others, which makes them amazing leaders. They are able to make the most of this invaluable information to strengthen their loyalty and forge stronger relationships with people. A competent leader is intuitively tuned in to the most compelling aspirations and desires of his followers. He knows the "hot buttons" of his employees and exactly how to channelize these "hot buttons" to increase overall productivity and positivity within the work environment.

Emotionally intelligent leaders know how to channelize this information for extracting better performance/productivity from people and keeping them happy. People with a high emotional quotient excel at recognizing the strengths and weaknesses of people and harnessing an individual's virtues for benefiting the team.

High emotional intelligence creates better leaders who are able to inspire greater faith and loyalty by using their teams or followers or emotional range. They are more aware of their emotions, which allows emotionally intelligent folks to create a harmonious environment. Practicing emotional intelligence makes you a better leader.

Did you know 67% of all competencies said to be fundamental for high performance in the professional sphere is emotional intelligence? Take the example of the world's most successful

CEOs. Amazon's Jeff Bezos passionately talks about getting right into the hearts of his customers in a 2009 YouTube video while announcing the company's Zappos acquisition.

When Howard Schultz of Starbucks was a child, his father lost a health insurance claim. This turned him into one of the most empathetic CEOs, who is well known for showing his employees thoughtfulness by offering generous healthcare rewards. Little wonder then that these folks are as successful as they are. They understand the emotional pulse of their employees and customers and can keep them emotionally gratified.

Emotional intelligence helps in building emotional maturity, boosting social intelligence, preventing relationship problems, enhancing interpersonal communication, helping control emotions, dealing with stress, influencing leadership, helping authorities make sound business change decisions, supporting staff and controlling resistance to change.

Chapter 2:

How to Bring About a Shift in Emotions

The million-dollar question is – is it really possible to change one's emotions?

With all its advantages, who wouldn't want high emotional intelligence? Who wouldn't want greater professional success, business potential, leadership skills, relationship gratification, humor, good health, positivity and happiness around them? Think about an antidote that beats stress, helps you form rewarding relationships with people and much more.

Take any coaching intervention program, and it will generally highlight some aspect of emotional intelligence in the name of interpersonal skills or social/soft skills. The most compelling reason for this is that, while intelligence quotient is tough to change, the emotional quotient can be acquired with sufficient training and consistent practice. So, the good news is that even if you do not consider yourself very emotionally evolved, there is plenty of scopes to boost your emotional quotient or regulate/manage your emotions with practice, training, and conscious effort.

The best part about enhancing your emotional intelligence is it can be practiced in your everyday life. For instance, if you are short tempered, start by showing greater empathy or being a more considerate listener.

Utilize Information About Emotions Effectively

Treat your emotions as vital data pieces that can help you view things from a more objective perspective. Avoid suppressing, combating, ignoring, fighting or being overpowered by your emotions. Treat it as an invaluable resource of information that can help you lead a more intentional, positive and rewarding life.

The primary objective of emotional awareness is to focus on our emotions and utilize them constructively to reach an intended or desired outcome. When you curb your emotions, you rob yourself the opportunity to learn and absorb information from them.

Rather than treating it as an overwhelming feeling, treat it as plain data that shapes your view of the world and leads you to act in a certain manner. When you embrace this information and learn from it, you have access to plenty of emotions that can be channelized for driving you in a positive direction.

Identifying, acknowledging and recognizing emotions as a form of data is integral to the process of self-awareness. Work with the information rather than attempting to defeat it. Learn to notice your emotions objectively without judging or fixing them.

Take Responsibility for Your Emotions and Actions

This can be one of the most challenging, yet productive tips to boost your emotional quotient. Your emotions originate from you and therefore, you are completely responsible for them.

People around you may be responsible for creating certain situations, but it is ultimately you who are in charge of your reaction to those situations. You may not always be able to control how others around you speak or behave. However, the way you react to their words and actions is something you have control over.

If you are hurt by someone and lash out, you are the one responsible for it. Get out of the mindset that "someone makes you do something." No one can make you angry; you are responsible for your own anger. No one holds the strings to your emotions. No one makes you do or feel anything.

Your reaction is completely your own responsibility. Your feelings can offer you important guidelines about your experience with different people along with your own requirements and preferences. However, your feelings and actions are no one's but your own responsibility.

Once you start accepting responsibility for your feelings and behavior, it becomes simpler to manage it in order to impact all spheres of your life positively.

If you hurt people, be gracious enough to accept it and apologize. Ignoring the person or not accepting the responsibility for your behavior is not a sign of high emotional intelligence. Your relationships will be much more positive and people will forgive you more easily if you make an honest attempt to set things right rather than live in denial land. Accepting your mistakes, apologizing and moving on is a sign of high emotional intelligence.

Focus on Building a Higher Emotional Quotient

Though our capacity to recognize and handle our own and other people's emotions is largely determined by childhood experiences, heredity, and other factors, it isn't rigid. We can alter our ability to comprehend and manage emotions over the long-term with the right coaching and dedication.

You can change, of course, however, the question is do you want to change? Are you willing to put in the effort required to be more emotionally intelligent? Sometimes, while you may successfully be able to manage your external emotions, you may still grapple with emotions you do not manage to display on the outside.

While some folks are naturally positive, calm and social, others can be plain grumpy, egoistic, shy or insecure. However, no trait is unchangeable. If you truly want to change an aspect of your personality, you can. Emotional intelligence naturally increases with age, without any intervention. This is the rationale behind the popular belief that people gain more maturity as they grow older. Overall, yes, it is possible to improve your emotional quotient over the long term with intervention, guidance, and regular practice.

Build Flexibility

Sometimes we get stuck in our own monotonous traps and become rigid and inflexible, which may impair our emotional intelligence. People with a highly developed emotional quotient know when to adapt and keep pace with newer techniques rather than getting stuck in an increasingly unproductive cycle. They know when how to adapt and manage their emotions according to the situation. Emotionally intelligent folks know when to adapt and shift perceptions.

Those who possess a highly developed emotional quotient are always open to newer experiences, challenging opportunities and a variety of adventures. Be open to change and shed the uneasiness and inhibitions attached with change.

Learn to decipher the consequences of your words and behavior. Emotionally intelligent folks pick their battles very selectively. They realize that peace and relationships are more valuable than being right.

When you learn to evaluate the consequences of your words and actions and demonstrate more flexibility and adaptability in your actions/words, you display high emotional intelligence. This isn't to be mistaken with letting people walk all over you. By all means, be assertive. However, know that it's not about being right or winning arguments all the time. Emotional intelligence is being perspective enough to realize what is worth fighting for and what is worth giving up.

Practice Assertiveness

Emotionally intelligent folks know the importance of setting appropriate boundaries to let people know where we stand. You have the right to disagree with people without acting in a disagreeable manner. Learn to say no without feeling guilty when you are not up to something or you find people taking advantage of you. Set your priorities and safeguard yourself from stress, harm, and duress.

Rather than using "you" followed by the accusation and putting people on the defensive foot, try making them more open to listening to and understanding your point. For instance, instead of saying "you should do this" or "you are xyx," try saying, "I feel really uncomfortable when you expect me to do this over my priorities" or "I strongly believe that I deserve recognition from the organization based on my consistent performance and contributions."

See what we did there? We aren't putting people on the defensive by pointing a finger at them and saying, "you did this" or "you are like this." We are being assertive and talking about our feelings without blaming anybody.

Stay Emotionally Honest

Be emotionally honest and transparent. You are not communicating genuinely if you shut yourself off from expressing emotions. If you say you are alright with a sorrowful face, you are being dishonest in your communication. When you practice being more real about emotions, it is easier for people to read it. It is always great to be able to be yourself and share your real feelings. It helps people know your feelings and understand where you are coming from. They trust you more, which sets the base for more rewarding relationships.

By all means, manage your emotions so as to avoid hurting others, but misleading others about your emotions or denying really deep emotions is not a sign of high emotional intelligence.

Practice Greater Empathy

Empathy is all about trying to understand why someone feels or acts in the way they do by putting yourself in their shoes. It is also being able to communicate this understanding to them more effectively. Empathy can also apply to your emotions and feelings.

Each time you notice yourself experiencing a specific emotion or behavior, try and think why you feel the way you do. You may not be able to figure it out at the onset, but pay close attention and you'll start receiving various answers you didn't notice earlier.

When someone is experiencing a rather strong feeling, ask yourself how you would feel in a similar scenario. Always be interested in what people say so you can respond in a more sensitive manner. It is always a good practice to ask questions and summarize what people say so you are clear, and people know you are actively listening to them.

When you put yourself in the other person's shoes, you reduce reactivity. For instance, if your child is resisting something you are telling him/her, try thinking it isn't easy for them to deal with peer pressure and academics. Think for a moment how it must be to be a young kid in the current competitive age.

If your manager is being demanding and difficult, think about the pressure of performance expectation they are dealing with at the hands of senior management. When you start thinking more objectively by considering where the other person is coming from, understanding and conflict resolution become much simpler.

Managing other's emotions requires maturity, skill, and tact. Does it start by being aware of exactly where you want the person to go? Do you want to lead them to feel happier, calmer, more aware, secure, vigilant or cautious, for instance? Once you realize how they are feeling and how to lead them there, you will know what to say and do.

We tend to forget how particular experiences feel; even if we've lived through it ourselves. You can only imagine how much perspective limiting it becomes if we've not experienced what the other person is going through. What is the best way to bridge this gap?

The nucleus of empathy lies in understanding the "why" among other things. Why does this person feel the way they do? What are they dealing with that I fail to see? Why do I experience different feelings than them? Explore your "whys" and you will be well on your way to better understanding the f others.

Being kind, considerate and helpful is one of the best ways of practicing emotional intelligence.

Cognitive Behavioral Therapy to The Rescue

Some techniques for managing emotions such as cognitive behavioral therapy for better psychological flexibility can work better than other methods. Since emotional intelligence is linked to human behavior, it can never be an exact science. The dynamics of human behavior, motivation, communication, and feelings will keep changing. You have to identify and evaluate what works for you. While behavioral therapy works wonderfully well for some people, others may find meditation or deep breathing more effective in calming their emotions.

Here are some tried and tested tips for being the ultimate emotions mastery ninja.

Avoid Labeling Feelings and Emotions

All your emotions are valid, including the not so positive ones. Avoid assigning labels and judging your emotions. When you judge your feelings, you inhibit your ability to experience them. When you cannot fully express or experience something, you prevent yourself from using these emotions more positively.

Each emotion you experience is a vital piece of information closely linked with what is happening around you and how it affects you. Without information about your emotions, you'd be left clueless about how to react to your emotions and manage them more effectively.

Connect negative feelings to events, but avoid judging them to gain a better understanding. For instance, if you feel envious, try and figure out what the emotions are conveying to you about the situation. Learn to experience positive emotions so you can recognize each opportunity to feel them to the fullest.

Identify Recurring Patterns

This is one of the best parts of gaining greater self-awareness. The human brain is known for its tendency to follow already established neural pathways than create new ones. The already set neural pathways may not always meet a constructive or positive purpose. The good news – you can change neural pathways that don't make positive contributions.

For example, when an individual gets angry, he/she may keep all their rage pent up rather than freely express it. This may become a dangerous pattern, and send wrong signals to the brain to keep continuing this pattern. Each time you feel overpowering rage, you'll bottle up your feelings instead of freely expressing them.

This will become an established emotional pattern. However, when you are aware of this pattern, you will come up with ways to respond to the situation rather than reacting on an impulse or curbing the emotion. However, responding to emotion can happen only once you identify a pattern.

Identify how emotions are built, and what triggers you into feeling specific emotions. There can be a predictable or recognizable pattern to it. If we are experiencing frustration, we are likelier to perceive the situation with greater negativity. Likewise, when we are consumed by fear, we are likelier to interpret an external stimulus or trigger as a threat.

Being aware of these pre-existing biases and their effect on our emotions through a pattern equips us to break patterns that don't serve us. The more you tune in to your biases, the lower will be your chances or misreading or being affected by triggers.

Respond Instead of Reacting

Reacting is a more unconscious and uncontrolled process that is a result of an emotional trigger. For instance, you snap when someone annoys you or you are already stressed due to another reason.

Responding, on the other hand, is more controlled and something you choose to do. You decide exactly how you behave in a given situation. For example, explaining to someone you are not feeling too good and that this isn't the best time to interrupt you, and that later you'd be in a much better position to give them a good hearing. You've simply chosen to deal with the situation in a more productive and less impulsive manner by taking control of your emotions.

Evaluate how your actions will impact others before acting. If your behavior will affect others, try and place yourself in their shoes. How are they bound to feel if you say or do something? Would you like to go through the experience yourself? If you have to take a particular action, can you help people in coping with its effects?

Mindfulness and Deep Breathing Help

Our emotions are physiologically experienced. When we experience anger, distress, disappointment and other emotions, they are visible through the body's physical reactions. Our body reacts involuntarily to the emotions at an evolutionary level. How will your body react if you suddenly spot a wild beast in your path? Some of the most common reactions will be a faster heartbeat, faster pulse, sweating, shaking limbs, shallower breathing and so on.

When we stay composed in the face of these seemingly overpowering emotions, our emotions change rapidly. When we combat physical stress symptoms, the mind automatically feels good. Every time you feel nervous, anxious or tensed, take a deep breath or practice meditation.

Tune in to your inner self and pay close attention to your feelings. How does it feel when oxygen enters your throat, lungs chest, diaphragm, and stomach? The idea is to focus on your feelings mindfully without judging. Stay in the present moment while acknowledging your feelings without judging them. Concentrate on the flow of air that enters and leaves your abdomen. Even a few deep breaths are enough to get you into a more positive mindset.

If you find your mind drifting away from the breath with several thoughts, gently acknowledge the emotion without judging it or letting it affect you. Acknowledge the thought, and let it pass, before drawing focus back to the breath. Stay in the present in a more intentional and purposeful manner! Avoid letting thoughts about the past or future occupy your mind and focus solely on the breath. Watch the change in your emotional frequency.

Practice mindfulness or focusing attention on the present in a nonjudgmental and intentional manner in all areas of life such as eating, walking and more. It will help you calm down (especially if you are a more emotional impulse driven person) and gain more clarity. The practice of mindfulness will also reduce your chances of being overwhelmed by damaging feelings and emotions.

Emotional Intelligence Can be Constantly Developed

Our emotional intelligence pathway originates within the brain going right down to the spinal cord. The primary senses are involved here and must go to the brain's front portion before you start thinking logically or rationally about an occurrence.

Emotions are generated in our limbic system, which is why our emotional response to an incident occurs before the rational mind gets involved. Emotional intelligence is based on efficient communication patterns between the brain's logical and emotional points.

Have you heard of plasticity? It is a term used by neurologists for describing the brain's ability to keep evolving and changing. The brain keeps growing newer connections as we acquire new skills. The change is slow, as the brain keeps developing more and more connections to boost its efficiency.

When you use various strategies for boosting emotional intelligence, you are actually letting the microscopic neurons (billions of them) lined between the emotional and logical centers of the brain to branch into smaller arms that touch other cells. This simply means, one cell can form more than 15,000 connections. The chain reaction signifies it is simpler for the brain to adapt to this new behavior in the long-term. Once the brain is trained with the help of emotional intelligence strategies, it becomes a habitual behavior/thought pattern.

Recognize Emotions Based on Physiological Signals

Our emotions impact us not just psychologically, but also on a physiological level. For instance, you may feel overpowering anxiety just before a presentation or an important meeting. What are the physiological signs of this anxiety or nervousness? There is an uncomfortable feeling in the stomach, the throat may become dry, you start sweating, your hands/legs start shaking and so on.

When we are excited or eagerly looking forward to something, our heart starts pounding faster! Haven't you experienced this just before meeting your crush or going on a date? Nervousness can cause stiff muscles, while fear can cause our pulse rate to increase.

Studies have revealed that we undergo specific physiological reactions while experiencing strong emotions. These physical reactions are closely associated with our state of mind, and occur when specific body parts are activated by certain emotions.

There are patterns of physical sensations closely connected with every one of six basic emotions we experience – namely happiness, surprise, sadness, fear, anger, and disgust. These overlap physiological sensations experienced by the body. For instance, numbed limb sensations can be connected with sorrow. Likewise, heightened limb sensations can be linked with anger. When there is an overpowering feeling of disgust, we begin to experience strange sensations in the throat, chest and digestive system. Similarly, fear surprise and amazement lead a strange feeling in the chest.

Tune in to Your Behavior

You can only manage your emotions more effectively if you are consciously aware of it. It starts by paying very close attention to your emotions and their impact on your behavior. Emotional awareness is one of the cornerstones of EQ.

Start noticing how you act when you experience specific situations, and how it affects your everyday life. Do these feelings impact your productivity? How about your communication with other people? Do your emotions pose a threat to your overall well-being, including your physical and emotional health? How do you react when you are extremely angry, happy or sad? Once you are consciously aware of your reactions to emotions, you will be able to wield better control over them and channelize them more productively.

Dive into Your Subconscious Mind

How can you gain a greater awareness of your subconscious emotions or feelings? Apart from deep breathing and mindfulness, let your thoughts wander freely and evaluate where they go. Pay close attention to your dreams. Are there any recurring symbols that can be closely connected with the current events in your life?

Keep a journal and pen next to your bed and write down the details you can recall about your most compelling dreams as soon as you are up. Analyze the emotions and patterns of these dreams, their symbolic references and the message they are trying to communicate. When you gain a thorough understanding of the emotions that dominate your subconscious mind, it becomes simpler to train your subconscious mind to guide your actions.

Sometimes, our conscious minds are unable to come with solutions we are faced with, which is why the phrase "sleep on it" originated. Our subconscious mind's functionality is at its peak when we are asleep. Ever wondered why many a time the solution to our problems strikes us when we are asleep? Or we wake up with a totally different perspective or solution much to our surprise? Our subconscious mind is ticking overtime when our conscious mind is resting. By tuning into our subconscious mind, we are tapping into our innermost emotional reserve to uncover our deepest feelings.

Utilize the Mental Pause Button

Use your mental pause button each time you find yourself on the verge of speaking or acting. Take a moment, breathe deeply and think before you respond. Whenever you feel tempted to type an elaborate mail in rage, stop and think if it is going to help resolve the issue or only make it worse. Each time you feel like screaming at someone or making a combustible comment on social media, apply the pause button.

When you consciously work on pausing before you speak or act, you get into the habit of thinking before acting or speaking in a manner that can worsen any situation. You learn to manage, control and tackle your emotions to handle any situation in a more constructive manner. When you learn to use this technique, you realize the button to your feelings and emotions is in your hands.

When you sense a challenge in controlling impulses, deal with it by quickly diverting your attention. Distract your thoughts by counting or concentrating on a pre-planned diversion. Your mind can be trained to shift thoughts or conversations fast.

Reduce Negative Personalization

When we feel negatively impacted by someone's behavior, do not rush into a conclusion. Tempting as it is to ascribe a negative reason for their behavior, try to gather a more holistic perspective of the circumstances before reacting. For instance, it is easy to think a friend isn't returning your call or message because he/she wants to avoid you.

However, they may also be busy or ill or in a dire situation. When we avoid ascribing negative reasons or personalizing people's behavior, we view them more objectively and with less hateful/judgmental emotions. The ability to overcome negative personalization of people's behavior is critical for boosting your emotional quotient.

Tune in to Verbal Clues

Some of the best indicators of our emotional condition are the physical signals our body gives us. You can develop a greater awareness of your emotions simply by tuning in to your physical sensations. You may feel a knot in your tummy while commuting to work, which can be a sign of high stress.

Similarly, when you are with someone you've recently started dating, and experience a too strong to ignore flutter in your heart, it could be an indication of having found the person who you'd like to spend the rest of your life with. Our body is constantly trying to communicate emotions we may not be aware of through physical sensations. Listening to these feelings and emotions signaled by the body helps process our emotions and reactions more efficiently.

Handle Differences Like A Pro

One of the best tips for developing high emotional quotient is mastering conflict management skills. Conflict resolution actually puts your emotional intelligence to practical use. Resolving differences and conflicts involves many aspects, including identifying feelings, a clear expression of thoughts, active listening, staying calm and coming up with a solution that diffuses the situation rather than escalating it. When we struggle to understand and control our feeling, we experience a sense of irritation, depression and erratic behavior patterns.

Conflicts only get magnified, making it all the more stressful to deal with. Once you recognize yours and others' emotions and learn to manage them, you enjoy a happier and more balanced life.

Be an Active Listener

During arguments or disagreements, we often listen not to understand, but to react and respond. When the other person is speaking, we are almost mentally constructing our own arguments to answer back or give back to them. This leads to even more conflict.

Dealing with conflict becomes more effective when you tackle issues in an assertive. yet respective manner without being defensive. When you listen empathetically, your own thoughts and emotions are taken into account. Listening actively and empathetically can help you shed toxic feelings building up in you.

Be assertive by all means, but also practice active listening to find that one point that can lead to resolution. Problem solution only happens when you understand where the other person is coming from and what they want. You can find a middle ground only when you tune into the words, feelings, and emotions of the other person, not just to give a fitting reply, but also to resolve the issue. Listening is all about putting the other person's words, thoughts, and feelings first.

Your opinion about people or events may not change. However, the time spent listening to the other person may just calm you and help you come up with a more positive or constructive response. It may help you see things from a different perspective and analyze the situation more objectively.

Decode Body Language

Try to gauge people's innermost emotions by tuning into their body language. Pick up clues about their emotional health by observing their body language. Sometimes people say something while their expressions and gestures convey the opposite or deeper truth, they aren't comfortable revealing. When you practice being more mindful of their body language, you tap into their true emotional fabric to adapt your responses and reactions. Sometimes people resort to less conspicuous ways of communicating their emotions.

For instance, a person may try saying something reassuring, but the high tone of their voice may defeat those words and indicate high stress. These are small, yet powerful indicators of people's behavior patterns and reading them correctly will give you the power to unlock others' emotional framework.

Psychometric tests and feedback

One of the most crucial aspects if you want to enhance your emotional quotient through any coaching intervention or self-practice program, is accurate feedback. People generally do not realize how others perceive them, especially people in senior management positions in organizations.

Though these folks are increasingly motivated, responsible and high on technical skills, they rarely take the time to pause and assess their behavior. In a nutshell, we do not possess a very accurate notion of how nice we come across as. Wishful thinking, misplaced optimism, and overconfidence can be factors contributing to this blind spot.

Generally, people tend to over-evaluate themselves in the niceness department. They believe they are nicer than they actually are. Any effort at increasing your emotional quotient must begin with gaining a thorough understanding of your strengths and weaknesses. Use valid and genuine assessment techniques like personality tests or accurate feedback to determine your success with developing a higher emotional quotient.

Practice Greater Light Heartedness

When you are more light-hearted and optimistic, it is simpler to capture the goodness of everyday situations and objects. Positivity results in greater emotional happiness and increased opportunities. People are forever looking to be around optimistic folks who come up with positive connections and possibilities. When you become more negative, you only concentrate on what can go awry rather than building strong resistance.

People with a more evolved emotional quotient know how to utilize wit and humor to make everyone feel happier, positive and safer. They know the art of using laughter to tide over tough times.

Be Open to Constructive Feedback and Criticism

One of the smartest ways to develop a higher awareness of your emotions is to be more receptive to feedback, suggestions, and criticism from others. For example, a friend may inform you he/she feels you aren't genuinely happy for his/her accomplishments. He/she senses strong feelings of envy in you each time he/she talks about their achievements. This can help you gain invaluable information about your emotions and triggers.

Emotionally intelligent people are receptive and open to the idea of receiving feedback and taking into consideration the other person's perspective. You may not agree with what the person says, but you'll still understand why the person is saying what they are saying.

However, emotionally intelligent folks are flexible and open enough to listen to constructive and objective feedback. This helps emotionally intelligent people identify and work on their weak spots. You are able to identify your triggers, actions, thoughts, and behavior more effectively.

Haven't you seen people actively soliciting feedback from others about themselves? It isn't simply to validate or gain acceptance. At times, it's a genuine way to understand their actions and emotions from the objective perspective of another person. It is an emotion meter that will help you gain a more unbiased view of your emotions while helping you manage them more effectively.

I had a friend who had the habit of being the center of attention at every social gathering. Over a period of time, he became more emotionally evolved and realized that it wasn't a trait to be proud of. He genuinely didn't want to come across as an attention seeker. He then urged his friends to call out his behavior politely and assertively each time we found him hijacking a conversation or trying to hog the limelight. This strategy works well if you are aware of your weaknesses and want to work on them.

Enlist the help of a family member, co-worker or friend to discreetly bring your actions to your notice. Get your managers or co-workers to offer you constructive suggestions about how you can overcome certain behavior or thought patterns. This will help you make the most of your strengths, and work on your weaknesses for boosting your overall emotional intelligence.

What are your emotional and behavioral core competencies? Are you more empathetic and compassionate? Are you a team player? Are you an inspiring leader and communicator? Take the help of people to identify your emotional strengths and weaknesses, and use this knowledge positively to manage your emotions, thoughts, and behavior more effectively.

Self-awareness is not a brief journey. It is a lifelong pursuit that keeps evolving to help you become a better person and enjoy more rewarding interpersonal relationships.

Avoid Complaining

One of the first steps towards boosting your emotional intelligence is to stop complaining. Shed the victim syndrome and know that the solution to your problem is well within your grasp. Emotionally intelligent people rarely blame others or their circumstances for the challenges in their life.

Instead, they search for matured ways to dissolve a relationship or talk to people who've wronged them in private. They also have a steady stream of effective coping mechanisms such as yoga, meditation, nature trips or simply venting their feelings by writing.

Stay Positive

How would you rate your happiness quotient on a scale of 1 to 10? Emotional intelligence originates from being happy and vice versa. They aren't simply happy because good things are happening to them, but because they are great at managing and taking control of their own happiness.

Happiness originates from within. A person who is capable of managing his emotions efficiently wakes up joyfully each morning. These people encounter challenges too, just like everyone else. However, they do not let these issues dampen their zest for positivity. Develop greater emotional intelligence by keeping your mind clear, avoid getting caught in destructive self-pity and take charge of your happiness. Emotional intelligence comes with being more positive and solution-oriented.

Happy people gain more appreciation and following from people to help them tide over tough times. They spread more happiness, live longer and come up with a constructive solution. It is a misconception that happiness is a result of material possessions.

Genuinely happy people are those who can manage their emotions well, spread happiness, and most importantly those who focus on giving rather than receiving. Emotionally intelligent people know that it costs zilch to be happy and yet the returns are invaluable.

Utilize Third Person Voice

Studies about managing our emotions have revealed that when we attempt to distance from our feelings and perceive them in an objective light, we develop greater self-awareness. Distancing from our feelings lends the process more objectivity. Each time you feel an overpowering urge to think, "I am terribly hurt or upset" try saying "John/Jill is terribly hurt or upset."

I know it sounds ridiculous. However, it will lead you to impersonalize the feeling just enough for gaining an unbiased understanding of it. Tone it down a bit if you like by saying something like, "I am experiencing sorrow" or "one of my emotions currently is sorrow."

Through these techniques, you are slightly alienating yourself from strong emotions to stay more balanced and composed. It is pretty much like dealing with your feelings as another bit of information rather than being overpowered by them. Every time you find yourself experiencing a powerful urge to react to an emotional impulse, take time to label the emotion. Later, refer to experiencing the emotion in the third person to move away from the emotion, and view it more objectively.

Chapter 3:
Managing Impulses and Delaying Gratification

Have you ever said something in anger and then regretted it immediately? Have you ever acted on an impulse or haste only to regret it soon after the act? I can't even count the number of people who have lost their jobs, ruined their relationships, nixed their business negotiations and blown away friendships because of that one moment when they acted on impulse. When you don't allow thoughts to take over and control your words or actions, you demonstrate low emotional intelligence.

Thus, the concept of emotional intelligence is closely connected with delaying gratification. We've all acted at some point or the other without worrying about the consequences of our actions. Impulse control or the ability to construct our thoughts and actions prior to speaking or acting is a huge part of emotional control. You are able to manage your emotions more efficiently when you learn to override impulses. Therefore, impulse control is a huge part of emotional intelligence.

Ever wondered the reason behind counting until 10 or 100 or 1,000 before reacting each time you are angry? We've all had our parents and educators counsel us about how anger can be restrained by counting up to 10 or 100. It is simple – while you are in the process of counting, your emotional level is slowly decreasing. Once you are done with counting, the overpowering impulse to react to the emotion has passed. This allows you to act in a more rational and thoughtful manner.

Emotional intelligence is about identifying these impulsive reactions and being able to regulate them in a more positive and constructive manner. Rather than reacting mindlessly to a situation, you are able to stop and think before responding. You choose to respond carefully over reacting impulsively to accomplish a more positive outcome or thwart a potentially uncomfortable situation.

Here are some powerful tips for delaying gratification and boosting your ability to manage emotions more effectively.

1. Have a clear vision for your future. Delaying gratification and controlling impulses or emotions becomes easier when you have a clear picture of the future. When you know what you want to accomplish in the next 5, 8, 10 and 15 years, it is easier

to keep the bigger picture in mind when small temptations arise.

Your "why" (the compelling reason for accomplishing a goal) will keep you sustained throughout the process of meeting the goal. Have a plan to fulfill your goal once you have a clear goal in mind. Identifying your goals and how you'll reach them will help you resist the temptation more effectively.

2. Make spending money difficult. If you are a slave of plastic money and online transactions, you are making the process of spending money too easy for your own good. Paying with cold, hard cash can make you think several times before spending. You'll reconsider your purchases when you pay with real money rather than plastic. Earmark a part of your salary into a separate saving account that you won't touch. Make access to that account difficult.

3. Find ways to distract yourself from temptations and eliminate triggers. For instance, if you are planning to quit drinking, take a different route back home from work if there are several bars along the way. Instead of focusing on what you can't do, concentrate on the activities you are passionate about. Surround yourself with positive people and activities that will help you

dwell on your goal. Avoid trying to fill your time with material goods.

4. Make a list of common rationalizations. Find a counterpoint or counter-argument for each. For example, you were angry for just 5 minutes or you are spending only ten dollars extra; tell yourself that 5 minutes of anger is 150 minutes a month wasted in anger or $3,000 extra spent throughout the year.

5. Use a combination of logic and emotions to make important decisions. Yes, if used correctly, your emotions can guide you into making the best decisions. However, emotions should be thought through carefully before making decisions based on them. In that sense, avoid making decisions based on initial emotional impulses. Stop and think before reacting and use the available emotional information to the best of your advantage.

By stopping in your tracks before making a decision, you are giving yourself a decent chance to think, feel and act in your best interests. Some of our soundest decisions are wielded by using a combination of emotion and logic. If you think before reacting, you are giving yourself a good chance of thinking and acting in your best interest.

Emotional responses also need logical or rational considerations while making important decisions or even guiding behavior patterns. Next time you feel the urge to scream at your manager, understand why he/she is stressed. He/she may be facing pressure from his/her supervisors or he/she may not be in his/her element owing to personal issues that are affecting them. Every time you feel the urge to react, step back and take a few seconds to consider your actions and their consequences. Take time to understand people and situations before determining your course of action.

In the above example, instead of screaming back at your manager, you can assertively communicate to them that you understand there is high pressure on them and you can assure him/her you are giving it your best and won't let him/her down. Before acting, stop (or hit the pause button) and think. Consider your feelings and emotions by weighing every possible option, and then determine the subsequent course of action. I like to go over feelings and emotions mentally before taking any action.

For example, if you find an otherwise productive and high performing worker stealing from the office, there are several ways to deal with the situation. You can turn him/her over to the police, and lose a high performing employee or threaten to act against them/sack them or sit down for a talk about what made them do what they did (or understand their reasons for stealing).

Before reacting in a more impulse driven manner, try and go through the results of all possible actions (do the pluses and minuses for each option) before reacting to wield more balanced, logical and rational decisions. Your reactions and decisions should be a consideration of both logic and emotions instead of knee-jerk reactions.

Chapter 4:
Overcoming Negative Emotions

Once you gain an understanding of your innermost negative emotions, it is easier to manage them. The relationships and professional we enjoy in our life are often a direct result of our ability to regulate our emotions. Managing your emotions is not just integral to the process of enjoying a harmonious relationship with yourself and others.

Here are some of the most powerful and proven secrets for overcoming negative emotions.

1. Embrace what can't be changed. There are many things around you that you can't control or change even though you'd like to. Accept it, and move on. Focus on the blessings, and appreciate the good things surrounding you. It is pointless to keep dwelling on things that are beyond our control. Too much complaining, cynicism, and criticism is an indicator of low emotional quotient and social adaptability.

Stay composed, and be more aware of things around you. Change what is possible, and accept what cannot be changed. Don't be hard on yourself for what cannot be changed or what is beyond your control. Instead, focus your energy and attention on what can be changed. For example, if you have a constantly nagging or egoistical boss putting you down, you may not be able to change his/her personality. However, you can control your reaction by staying unaffected by his/her behavior or move jobs. This is critical to the process of developing greater emotional intelligence.

2. Ditch the victim mindset. You can't have a high emotional quotient and play victim all the time. The two just don't go along. Emotionally intelligent folks rarely play victims of people and circumstances. They are mature enough to accept responsibility for their thoughts and actions. One of the biggest challenges people face when it comes to boosting emotional intelligence is getting rid of the victim mindset.

Understand that the solution to the challenges you are facing is not outside but within you. You won't accomplish much by holding other people or circumstances responsible for things that happen to you. Break free from the victim mindset today and start accepting responsibility for your actions. The solution to almost every problem we face is within us. When we don't have the power to control or influence our circumstances, we can control our reaction to it.

Emotionally intelligent people do not engage in shifting the blame on other people or situations by playing the role of helpless victims. Their approach is more proactive when it comes to changing aspects within their realm of control. There are mature enough to deal with or accept things that can't be changed and take control of things that can be changed. People with high emotional intelligence understand their limitations, which lets them accept and deal with their shortcomings.

Emotionally intelligent people seldom play victims. One of the fundamental steps for boosting your emotional quotient is giving up the victim mindset or syndrome. Realize that the solution to your problem is within you. Even when we cannot control our circumstances, we can control our reaction or responses to it.

Emotionally intelligent folks do not shift the blame to other people or circumstances. They are more proactive when it comes to changing things that can be changed and mature enough to accept things that can't be changed. People with increased emotional quotient realize their limitations, which allow them to accept their shortcomings.

3. Use stop-drop method. Each time you find yourself overcome by compelling emotions or have the urge to succumb to stressful feelings and emotions, grab a pen and paper and note down your emotions in a detailed and comprehensive manner. Ensure the emotions and feelings are clearly mentioned and acknowledged.

If you've been raised in the 90s, you may be well-acquainted with the now redundant VCR models. Remember the big and conspicuously placed pause button. This is how you are going to operate your negative thoughts, feelings, and emotions from now on. Press the "pause" button when you find your thoughts and feeling running unleashed. Focus the attention of the heart as the point from which all your feelings and emotions originate.

Think of something exceptionally wonderful or beautiful that you experienced recently. It can be a gorgeous sunset or the blue waters you witnessed on one of your trips. It can be a thriving garden, a cute baby, or a puppy you spotted in the neighborhood. Anything that evokes positive feelings, experiences and emotions within you! The goal is to switch or transform your emotional frequency from negative to positive.

Allow the feelings and emotions to stay within you for some time. Concentrate on positive feelings, and the experiences brought about by these feelings in your heart and entire being.

If letting go of negative emotions still seems like a challenge, accompany these thoughts with long and deep breaths. Hold positive thoughts or feelings, and allow them to linger for a while. Acknowledge the positivity and goodness without feeling pressurized to replace the so-called negative feelings or emotional impulses.

Press the pause button mentally and revisit compelling feelings and emotions. How do they appear now? How do you feel about these potentially negative feelings and emotions currently? Write everything down like you are experiencing it or mention all the thoughts, feelings and emotions occupying your mind. Now, act on the new wave of feelings if they feel more suitable. If you still feel an overpowering sense of negativity, use the stop drop method all over again.

The entire process will make it easier for you to resist succumbing to your impulses or emotional reactions. Bring about a shift in your thoughts, actions, and mindset without undermining or suffocating your feelings. The more you try to forcibly curb your thoughts, the greater will the force with which they return. Bring about a gentle shift in your feelings and emotions.

The objective is to acknowledge these feelings in an unbiased manner and allow them to pass without being affected by them. When our emotions transform, the brain invariably aligns with it. This is exactly how our actions start becoming more value and purpose-driven than uncontrollable emotional impulses.

4. Shift focus on your strengths. Concentrating on your strengths is one of the best ways to deal with negative emotions. Indulge in more of what you do will to develop a more positive, balanced and inspired mindset, which eventually makes it simpler to manage overpowering emotions. This helps us keep increasing stress levels and depression at bay. Finding the balance and regulating emotional behavior is easier when you tune in to your strengths.

5. Talk to a trusted person. Another way to manage negative emotions is to gather unbiased feedback from a trusted aide, friend or family member. Seeking professional help will also help you gain a comprehensive understanding of your emotions and feelings.

6. Exercise, exercise, and exercise. Exercise is a wonderful way to release our brain's dopamine chemical, which helps us experience a sense of elation, positive, reward and pleasure. It's a feel-good hormone that will put you in a naturally positive and happy state of mind. This ultimately makes you less irritable and more restrained when it comes to regulating emotions.

7. Show gratitude. Develop the habit of appreciating blessings instead of whining about things. Appreciate and express gratefulness for everything people do for you instead of taking it granted. Thank people frequently. Be grateful for everything you have. At the end of your day, list all the things in your life or that happened during the day for which you are thankful. It can be driving to work in your car or the feet you've been blessed to work on or the roof over your head.

There are plenty of things to be thankful for. Counting your blessings is one of the best ways to notice the positives around you, and increase your positive thinking frequency. Make a list of new blessings each day, and you'll realize just how much you have to be thankful for.

8. Speak about negative emotions. Spend time talking about your feelings and connecting with people rather than brooding or ruminating over your emotions. If you keep thinking about it, you are likely to view these negative emotions in a unidimensional manner based on your perspective.

However, by talking about it with a trusted person who knows you well, you are considering these emotions from another perspective, which may help you understand them with a more open and broader outlook. Build connections with people to understand and manage your emotions more effectively.

9. Apply balanced thinking in a majority of situations - One of the biggest reasons we find it challenging to cope with or regulate our emotions is because we engage in catastrophic thinking (thinking in terms of black and white or extremes) instead of thinking in balanced or grey terms. Avoid giving in to negative thinking. Challenge your monstrous inner critic, and move your thought or emotional frequency from negative and damaging to positive and constructive.

Every time you feel overwhelmed by negative thoughts, undertake physical activities such as snapping rubber bands on the wrist, biting your tongue or pinching yourself. Once you do this, watch out for evidence that questions your negative thoughts. The objective is to look out for evidence different from your beliefs, thoughts or emotions.

Let us for instance see that your spouse isn't responding to your calls and messages. There is a surge of involuntary and compulsively negative feelings and emotions that make their way into our minds such as "he/she doesn't care about me" or "they are having an affair with someone else and hence avoiding my call."

Each time you feel yourself thinking in terms of extremes, look for evidence that challenges this negative thinking. Go back to all the times they have quickly responded to your calls and messages and demonstrated they care about you. Avoid engaging in catastrophic thinking. Develop a more rational and balanced thought process. Things are often not as bad or negative as we imagine them to be. Develop the habit of consciously gathering evidence in support of your balanced thinking. This will increase your ability to perceive the situation more positively.

Practice neutral thinking or avoid thinking in terms of black and white. Balanced thinking can be developed over a period of time by changing the frequency of our thoughts from negative to positive or neutral. A majority of us tend to think in terms of extremes, which needs to change with consistent implementation of this strategy and thought training.

10. Avoid becoming a hostage of destructive thinking. Learn to challenge your inner critic and move the frequency of damaging and destructive thoughts to positive and constructive. Each time you feel overwhelmed by a negative thought, perform a physical action (like snapping a rubber band on your wrist or pinching yourself). Once that's done, look for evidence that challenges your negative thought patterns. The idea is to challenge this negative feeling by looking for evidence contrary to what you believe.

For example, if your partner hasn't responded to your message, instead of thinking he/she doesn't give a damn about your feelings or is busy with someone else, gather evidence against this negative feeling. Think of all the times he/she has promptly responded to your message, demonstrated care affection and been around during tough times. Avoid catastrophic thinking or thinking in terms of extremes. Develop a more thoughtful process. Many times things aren't as bad as we imagine them to be. Consciously build the habit of gathering evidence against negative thinking to increase your capacity to perceive the situation in a more positive manner.

11. Show kindness, consideration, and compassion. Extending kindness, thoughtfulness, and compassion to other people frees you from the clutches of stress and negativity. When doing random or well-thought acts of kindness for others, you feel a greater sense of well-being and gratification within yourself, which is important for stress reduction and managing difficult emotions.

By giving and showing kindness, we develop a greater appreciation for what we have, which in turn helps our positive thinking. We also become more accepting and accommodating of people around us. The thought that you've made a small difference to someone's life can quickly skyrocket your positive emotions.

12. Divert attention from negative or overwhelming emotions.
Mentally switch yourself from negative thoughts and focus on interesting and fun distractions such as watching your favorite comedy show or movie, reading an inspiring book, browsing through humorous comic strips and surfing the internet for fun videos. It's a wonderful way to switch your mind's frequency from negative to positive and feel good.

This shouldn't be seen as an act of running away from your emotions. You are merely on a break from them so you can reorganize your thoughts, feelings, and emotions, and later check to see if you feel any differently about the issue or situation. At times, our earlier, impulse-driven reaction varies from how we perceive the situation later. Taking a break from our feelings gives us the ability to gauge the intensity of our feelings, and determine if we feel the same as our initial reaction.

This is another killer mechanism when it comes to dealing with your feelings and emotions more effectively. Visualize a big red button in the middle of your forehead. This is the button you will use to bring about a quick shift in your thoughts from negative to positive. Each time you want to switch your thoughts or bring about a shift in your emotions, gently touch the middle of your forehead as if activating the big red button that flips the channel of your mental imagery and draws you into the more positive and fulfilling frame of mind. It is similar to flipping channels you don't want to watch or radio station you don't want to hear.

Keep switching off from negative and destructive thoughts to positive feelings and emotions. Focus on something fun and interesting such as watching your favorite movie, reading a fun book, catching a show at the comedy club, reading funny comic strips and so on. The objective is to bring about a shift in your emotions from negative to positive and feel wonderful.

I know some of you may view this as a way of escaping our emotions. Understand that you are not running away from your feelings or emotions. Instead, you are simply taking a break to realign your thoughts and feelings in a more balanced way. After a while, check to see if you feel any differently where these feelings, thoughts, and emotions are concerned.

Sometimes, we are so driven by our emotional impulses that it becomes challenging to keep things in perspective. We don't focus on the bigger picture. Instead, we view the situation or person from a narrower and negative perspective. Taking a break from your emotions and feelings gives you the ability to determine the intensity of your emotions, and gauge if you still feel the need to respond in the manner you did earlier.

Think of it like this. When a relationship is not working out for us, we don't immediately end it, do we? At times, we just decide to take time off from it and gauge if we still have similar feelings for the person. We live away from the person for a while and take stock of life without the person. Once we realize our true feelings for the person, we either decide to end the relationship or reconcile with him/her.

You are using pretty much the same technique with your emotions. You aren't breaking ties with them or running away from them. You are simply taking a break to analyze them to see if you still feel the need to react in as compelling a way as you did earlier.

A majority of the time, our initial reaction is nothing but an impulse. It isn't a well-thought or contemplated decision that arises from balanced thinking or keeping your eyes fixed on the larger picture.

Taking a break from our feelings and emotions gives us the power to think through these feelings and emotional impulses in a more balanced or neutral manner. Going on a break from your feelings offers you to the ability to contemplate the intensity of your feelings and emotions, and determine if you feel as strongly about it later as you did about the emotion originally.

Keep fixated on the larger picture or perspective to bring about a positive alignment in your emotions. Every situation in our life is geared for filling a higher purpose, even the most seemingly negative situation. It may not be obvious at the outset, however real emotional maturity and intelligence involve perceiving a situation from a broader perspective.

Even when you cannot comprehend the real importance of a situation, in the beginning, you'll understand its significance of the lesson once it unfolds over a period of time. Sometimes, all we require is a simple shift in perspective to view a seemingly challenging or negative situation in a more positive or constructive light.

13. Utilize mantras and affirmations to program your subconscious. This is one of the most powerful techniques when it comes to bringing about a shift in your thoughts, feelings, and emotions at a subconscious level for managing your emotions more effectively. Every time you experience a compelling urge to give in to your emotions, mentally or verbally recite a mantra, slogan, quote or affirmation. This not just helps align our thoughts to experience greater positivity but also brings about a change at a subconscious level over how we think and act over a period of time.

Our subconscious mind is a highly potent tool and can be used to fulfill almost any desire or goal. When you keep feeding a particular idea or thought into it, the subconscious mind doesn't believe it to be aspirational thinking. It accepts the wishful thinking as your reality. For instance, if you say you are a "happy, positive and prosperous person" even when you aren't, the subconscious mind accepts this affirmation as your reality once it has been repeated for a while.

There isn't a way of the subconscious mind to differentiate between reality and imagined reality or wishful thinking.

Whatever enters its realm repeatedly becomes its reality. Once the subconscious mind accepts a certain idea or affirmation as your reality, it directs your actions in line with this reality. Thus, you will be driven or guided towards actions that are in alignment with the affirmations, eventually making them your reality. This information can be used to manifest pretty much everything you want in life not just greater emotional intelligence.

I'd recommend creating your own unique, personalized and meaningful mantra or affirmation. Make it more intentional, purposeful and thoughtful with mantras such as, "I feel happy, positive, fulfilled and content" or "I feel emotionally balanced and good. This is change is for the better."

Find more constructive releases for your feelings and emotions. Allowing emotions to build up can be stressful, destructive and unhealthy. Develop hobbies and creative pursuits (painting, woodworking, knitting, sculpting, gardening and more) as healthy outlets for releasing accumulated potentially negative energy.

There are people who've admitted to feeling a huge surge of relief from negative emotions by practicing more action-oriented and energetic disciplines like kick-boxing and taekwondo. It brings about a catharsis of sorts. While some people engage in more aggressive sports and pursuits for releasing their pent-up negative energy, others take to mantra chanting, meditation or yoga for freeing themselves from the shackles of unwanted thoughts, feelings, and emotions.

14. Avoid blowing things out of proportion. Picking battles wisely is critical to the process of managing our emotions. If you fight for everything, you'll end up with nothing. If we don't choose our battles wisely, we end up frustrated, stressed, disappointed and confused. At times, it's best to let go. Each time a challenging situation arises, question yourself how crucial or urgent it is before getting into panic or combat mode.

The human mind, since evolution, is trained to blow things out of proportion. We tend to imagine the worst even when things aren't as bad as they appear. For leading a happier, more emotionally balanced and less stressful life, learn to let small matters pass. You don't have to react to everything.

15. Follow the empty chair technique - This technique is a widely utilized gestalt therapy for helping a person shift their thoughts or mindset through conversation with an imagined person. The participant engages in roleplay with an imaginary ally, family member or other individual sitting opposite them on an empty chair. This is why it is referred to as the empty chair technique. The aim of the technique is speaking about feelings and emotions that you wouldn't normally talk about to anyone in person.

For example, let us assume you are jealous of a friend for having it all or being more successful or richer than you. This invariably leads to you developing hatred for him/her. Looking at it objectively, you realize that the feelings aren't a result of their actions but a culmination of your negative perceptions about their success when compared to yours. Obviously, this isn't something you are comfortable sharing with him/her owing to the risk of losing their friendship.

The objective is to accomplish some type of emotional catharsis by opening your feelings and emotions to the friend in an imaginary way. This helps you deal with the emotion more effectively. At times, people engage in the empty chair technique as a rehearsal before actually talking to a person about a tricky or sensitive topic. It helps the person muster enough courage and regulate their emotions more efficiently. The role of the person you can speak can be played by your therapist or another person too.

16. Use suitable outlets for releasing negative emotions. Building up emotions can be destructive, unhealthy and stressful. Develop hobbies and creative pursuits such as painting, knitting, gardening, sculpting and more to develop a healthy outlet for releasing pent up emotions. Speaking to someone you trust, getting an unbiased view from a trusted person and seeking professional help you develop a good understanding of your feelings. I know several people who find practicing aggressive disciplines such as kickboxing cathartic. Still, others turn to meditation and mantra chanting for liberating themselves from accumulated negative emotions.

17. Spend more time outdoors. By spending time outdoors, you are opening your mind, body, and spirit to a fresh supply of oxygen. Fresh air can do your body and brain a whole lot of good. The fact that nature is soothing and therapeutic is no secret. Each time you find yourself overwhelmed by emotions, go for a long walk in the woods. Natural beauty and resources are known to calm our spirit and make a positive impact on the way we feel. Plonk yourself up a lush green hill or neighborhood park to engage in some positive, feel-good nature therapy.

18. Manage your impulses. One of the most crucial aspects of developing higher emotional intelligence is to consciously work towards overcoming distraction, developing a more analytic approach towards impulses and creating coping strategies. Each time you come across a situation with overpowering impulses, count backward from ten to one or concentrate on distraction thoughts set in advance.

Keep a set of thoughts aside as your distraction thoughts. Every time you feel the urge to react your impulses, go back to your distraction thoughts. Train yourself to shift thoughts quickly or change the conversation topic. Don't be sucked into a conversation that triggers negative or potentially destructive emotions in you.

Analyze your feelings, thoughts, and emotions rationally each time you experience a feeling of impulsiveness. Question yourself about why you are focusing on a stressful problem or situation. Ask yourself how thinking or ruminating on the issue is beneficial for you. Should your mind be occupied with other feelings? What are the most suitable alternatives for these thoughts and impulses?

A lot of people who are working towards increasing their emotional intelligence create a coping strategy that involves utilizing a set of pre-determined thoughts that help combat impulses. These coping thoughts can include positive affirmations such as "I am completely in control of my emotions, feelings, and thoughts" or "I do not have to respond to the emotion immediately" or something similar.

Affirmations help reinforce the idea within your subconscious mind, which directs your actions to refrain from reacting to the impulse immediately. Have your own coping mechanism in place in the event a strong emotional impulse strike. This may not come immediately. However, with consistent training and practice, you'll acquire the art of managing your impulses and reactions.

Do not react to the emotional impulse right away. If you give in to it immediately, you'll most likely do or say something you'll regret once the impulse dies down. Balance the overwhelming emotional impulse.

Chapter 5:
Building Self-Esteem

So, it sounds very good, loving yourself, appreciating and accepting yourself and taking the responsibility for your happiness in your own hands. How do you actually go about doing it? Is self-esteem a mere concept or are there workable techniques that can be followed consistently to put it into practice on a daily basis? Can we lead a truly glowing life if we take time out consciously to practice increasing self-esteem? Well, give yourself a big hug, grab your favorite cookies and read on.

1. Avoid comparisons. No one is the universe is like you. You're one of a kind and it's not fair to compare yourself with anyone else. The only justified comparison is with yourself.

2. Treat all with love, compassion, and respect. You will feel way better about yourself when you treat others in a way you want to be treated. Not everyone will reciprocate your kindness of course, but that's really not your problem, is it?

3. Get real. All of us have our happy and sad moments and it's not possible to be all glowing happy every single day. There

will be tough days, we will make mistakes, and there will be setbacks and negative emotions. Let yourself be human enough to experience all of this as well.

4. End all toxic relationships. You don't deserve anyone who doesn't love you for the amazing person you are or doesn't make you feel special.

5. Create a list of all the positive things in your life. You will only learn to love yourself when you truly come to appreciate all the gifts you are bestowed with. Just maintain a journal or 'happiness book' and keep writing everything that's going fantastically in your life. The positivity will transform the way you feel about yourself and your life.

6. Allow yourself to be guided by intuition. Look out for signs that award you a positive gut feeling. Make a conscious effort to tune in to your inner voice while making important decisions. These inner voices will always guide you and reinforce your self-love.

7. It is alright to enlist the help of others when you're going through challenging times. It can be anyone from a family member to a friend to healer and support group. It's not always brave to tide through tough times alone.

8. Display gratitude. Find something that makes you feel grateful on a daily basis. There are going to be bad days, and on these days it's especially important to count your blessings. It will shift the energy from what you don't have to everything you are blessed with.

9. Start every day with positive affirmations. It can be anything short and sweet that resonates with your persona. It can be anything from how wonderfully you tackled a situation recently or how healthy you feel or how amazing you look. Anything that makes you feel good about yourself

10. Express your creativity by doing whatever makes you happy. It can be paining, music, knitting, sculpting, gardening, writing or anything similar that helps you release your productive energy and makes you feel great about yourself.

11. Get out of your comfort zone to accomplish something new. The feeling of trying and succeeding in something unknown makes us realize we are capable of much more than we give ourselves credit for.

12. Consume healthy food and drinks. Few things define loving yourself and building a higher sense of self-esteem as graciously as a body that is well-nourished and well-tended to.

13. Acknowledge and wholeheartedly embrace the qualities that make you differ from others. Remember, this is what defines your specialty. This is what sets you apart from the rest of the pack.

14. Come up with a nurturing self-love ritual. It can be anything from lovingly moisturizing yourself to enjoying a bubble bath. Switch off your electronic gadgets, tune out of social media, and enjoy your self-love ritual regularly whenever you find the time.

15. Know that physical beauty is impossible to define as per a set criterion, as airbrushed beauty magazines will have you believe. The motion of beauty depends on how you perceive it. You are beautiful. Every person is beautiful in their own way. Cherish your body and physical beauty and learn love it unconditionally.

16. Run after your passion relentlessly. You know exactly what you want but there are plenty of feelings of self-doubt and fear that keep you from fulfilling your dreams. If you really want to do something, stop thinking it won't work and just get up and do it.

17. Clear your closet. This goes beyond being simply therapeutic. Cleaning out unwanted objects frees up the clogged energy within your space and mind and has a positive impact

on you. The negative vibrations of elements that are not needed in your life can consume your energy wastefully.

18. Surround yourself by a happy and supportive set of people who motivate you and have your best interests in mind. We can't always choose the people we're with, but wherever you can (friends, family, support groups, clubs), know that you deserve to be around folks who love you for what you are. They will have an innately positive impact on building your positive emotions and self-esteem.

19. Jot down your goals and be mindful of what you want to accomplish in life. This will help you manifest these goals to live the life of your dreams.

20. Celebrate your accomplishments. Yes, every single one of them merits a celebration. Even if it's something small, don't forget to reward yourself for it. Be proud of your achievements, irrespective of whether others are.

21. Stay perseverant and patient. Building high self-esteem is not an easy process. It keeps developing and takes time to conquer. Stay kind to yourself through tough times and keep motivating yourself.

22. Do not be a 'yes person'. It's alright and in fact, recommended that you don't say yes to everything that people

ask of you. It's perfectly fine to say no when you mean and feel no. It doesn't make you a shoddy person, only a smart person who knows about his/her priorities.

23. Pick up new skills. Few things can pump up your confidence like acquiring new skills and abilities. Keep striving to learn new things and skills within and outside your domain of work. It can be practicing yoga or learning a foreign language or learning how to cook or sing.

When you develop new skill sets regularly and are capable of multitasking and managing multiple functions with ease, it automatically elevates your self-confidence. Challenge yourself constantly by setting up new targets and goals.

24. Take a break from your busy schedule each morning to practicing deep breathing exercises to tune in with your inner self.

25. Take some time out by grabbing your favorite wine or coffee and relax, without any outward distractions. Just think about all the fabulous things happening in your life and how you want your life to shape up in the future.

26. Don't allow your inner critic to rear its ugly head periodically. While some feelings of self-doubt are natural, don't believe all the things you think very seriously. Sometimes, we're

just too hard on ourselves and lack the objectivity perspective when judging ourselves.

27. Forgive yourself. This is an extremely aspect of accepting yourself unconditionally. You need to be able to let go of the things you did in the past that you aren't particularly proud of. Don't seek to change or undo anything. Just learn from your past mistakes to create a better future.

28. Recognize your happy and positive place. Is there a place that gives you a really positive aura? Any place that makes you feel happy, calm and peaceful? Does that boost your feel-good quotient? Take yourself to that place either physically or mentally when you're down and see the effect it has on you. Visualize yourself experiencing the place through your senses feel a sense of positivity rush through you.

29. Engage in a healthy dialogue with yourself. Talk to yourself in a loving, motivating, empathetic manner; the same way you'd talk to a close friend or family member. You deserve the kindness and empathy you give others too.

30. Explore your spirituality. Faith is the true basis of loving yourself. You need to strongly believe in a force (whether the universe or a god) to explore the beauty of your soul. Spirituality takes an individual on a never-ending journey of

discovering things about oneself in the form of feelings, raw emotions and underlying thoughts.

31. Get rid of past baggage. This may not be as easy as it sounds. Healing from a past wound may require some support from others, along with time and a conscious effort on our part. But for your own sake, since you don't really deserve to carry the burden around all the time, learn to let go of it gradually. You know you don't deserve to live with it all your life.

32. Exercise. Move that body each day so you feel fit, fine and great about yourself. This isn't to reinforce the belief that a thin or sculpted body is the best. It is to keep yourself active, healthy, energetic and always pumped up.

33. Take tiny steps. It is unrealistic to expect yourself to go from low self-esteem to high self-esteem in a day. You need to understand it's a gradual process that will happen with tiny improvements and achievements over a span of time. Don't get bogged down by negative thoughts.

Identify why you are developing negative thoughts and eliminate them with the right tools instantly. Find out why you feel the way you do and resort to corrective action immediately to help you stay in line with your goal of building high self-esteem.

34. Surrender Yourself to Service. Find small ways to contribute to your community. When you offer service, assistance, and kindness to others, it will help you feel complete and fulfilled within yourself.

35. Do something you have never had the courage to. No, this isn't just true for your larger than life movies. It works wonderfully in real life too. Once we conquer our fear and achieve something that we've always been afraid of, it skyrockets our confidence. The newer and more daring things we try, the more we believe in our ability to put off things which we had thought impossible till some ago. Sometimes, we have to push ourselves to convince ourselves what we are capable of.

36. Have a blast. Have fun and do all the things that light up the fire within you. Enjoy doing it and lead the amazing life you're meant to lead.

37. Set Goals - According to a research experiment conducted at Virginia Tech, people who consistently jot down their goals make nine times as much money over their entire lifetime as people who simply don't take the trouble of writing their goals. Once you write down your goals, you internalize it and your actions are completely in sync with achieving the goals. Your

confidence automatically soars once you set goals and go about achieving your goals regularly.

38. Enlist professional help whenever required. Whether it is therapy, counseling, medication or anything else you need to get out of a tough situation, go out there and enlist the help of professionals to help tide you over during difficult times.

39. Take away focus from perfection and focus on accomplishing tasks. Take away your focus from attaining the ultimate level of perfection and pay heed instead on undertaking small accomplishments. It's not sensible to be hard on yourself in a bid to boost your self-esteem. No one is perfect. You're not going to sport a near perfect body or have a perfect house or the perfect kids.

Don't bathe in the concept of perfection all the time. There is so much emphasis on the idea of perfection in the media that we tend to lose ourselves trying to be everything they tell us we should be or is the ideal. Stop following beauty magazines that make you feel ugly. Stop reading books that talk about perfect relationships. It is a highly artificial concept driven by a consumerist economy.

Instead hold on to your achievements, however small they may seem. Acknowledge that not everyone can pull off what you do and that you're special for the way you do it. Recognize the actual value of your achievements rather than simply brushing them aside as easy and inconsequential.

Write down a list of everything you've achieved within the day on a daily basis. Just like connecting the dots game, your small accomplishments every day will help you achieve the bigger picture in life gradually.

Each goal will lead you on to another and take you a step closer to your final goal. This journey will also include making mistakes and you will have to be able to accept your mistakes as part of a never-ending learning process. Mistakes don't make you an inferior person. They contribute to an opportunity to learn and grow. For every mistake you make, you learn of a new way to not do things in the future. Makes sense? Avoid being trapped in the self-pity and negativity syndrome, and strive for excellence over perfection.

40. Life others to life yourself. Help somebody feel wonderful about themselves by teaching them a skill or something that boosts their confidence. It's not rocket science. When you help others feel wonderful about themselves, you automatically feel amazing about yourself. Find ways to make others feel great about themselves or to bring a smile on their face. You will feel

super confident when you realize you have the power to make a positive difference in people's lives.

41. Do not complain all the time. Understanding that everyone has problems and that they can handle with positivity, patience and perseverance is an important aspect of being a confident person. People with high self-esteem take control of the situation proactively and don't play victims in challenging situations. They don't award control to the situation, but take things in their own hands to tackle the situation.

Confident people don't get overwhelmed by tough times. They realize that though they can't control everything that comes their way, they can control their reaction to it. Proactively being in control of any challenging situation rather than simply playing a reactive victim soars our confidence by several levels and increases our ability to deal with tough situations.

42. Build a powerful vision. Use the power of visualization and imagination to boost your self-confidence. Imagine yourself to be the perfectly self-assured and self-confident person that you truly want to be. How do feel internally when your imagine yourself to be this person? How do you think others will see you? How will you feel, act, think and talk? Utilize the force of

the mind's eye to experience these feelings from the perspective of a confident person.

You can do this exercise daily for 10-15 minutes at the beginning of the day. Put on some music to relax you, and once you're done, right down everything you visualized in a specially created journal.

43. Socialize- Yes, self-esteem and self-confidence stems from self-love and accepting yourself unconditionally. However, it doesn't hurt to go out there and socialize with like-minded people who radiate an encouraging aura. Connecting with positive, inspiring and motivating people will not just help you absorb their powerful mindset, but also give you an opportunity to enhance your communication and social skills.

44. Direct your nervous energy towards constructive pursuits. Nervousness can actually be good for you. It drives up the adrenaline and makes you feel more alert. The added energy can be utilized wonderfully to create positive things.

If you're a nervous wreck just before an all-important presentation, use up your entire extra nervous energy to communicate with even more enthusiasm and intensity. You may be surprised at what you are capable of achieving when you're nervous. And once you manage to pull it off successfully, your self-esteem will get a much-needed boost.

45. Do a SWOT analysis. SWOT analysis is a concept followed by businesses to identify their strengths, weakness, opportunities, and threats to foster a more efficient decision-making process.

You can use this brilliant technique to carry out a SWOT analysis of yourself. Think about what you and others think are your strengths and weaknesses. Work out what opportunities and threats can be experienced based on these strengths and weaknesses.

Take time to reflect on your wonderful strengths. Contemplate how you can overcome your weaknesses. Enlist the help of others, if required, to conquer your weaknesses.

Is there anything you can do to improve your communication skills? Can you develop your social skills? What can you do to enhance your organization skills? Identify areas that need improvement in your life and that are stopping you from being the spectacular person you are, and work on it consciously and continuously. Commit yourself to achieve success with a thorough analysis of your personality.

46. Keep self-criticism constructive and positive. The objective of self-criticism is not to belittle yourself by emphasizing your weaknesses, but to be completely aware of your strengths and weaknesses to guide your actions fruitfully. When we take stock of your limitations and virtues, we gain greater awareness about ourselves. Positive self-criticism helps us accept our limitations and work around them by highlighting our positives.

Self-criticism need not always be how poorly you performed or how you can never match up to others. It is all about gaining deeper insights into yourself to help you determine the positives that will help you live a life of your dreams, and facilitate more positive emotions. Self-critiquing is about molding your personality in a way that facilitates achieving self-goals. It also means working on those qualities that may obstruct your goal fulfillment.

Whenever you find yourself indulging in the self-critical talk, keep it balanced and positive. Think about how you can work on your weaknesses and replace them with your positives rather than constantly thinking about how bad you are. All you need is a shift in words and perception. When you change the emphasis from I am not good enough to do this to how can I use my positives to do this, it can bring about a severe change in the manner with which you approach the task.

47. Keep the motivation flame burning. There's nothing quite like feeding yourself a daily dose of motivation to stay popped up always. Read something positive and inspiring that can lift your spirits. Watch motivational videos, listen to the talks of popular motivational leaders, go through favorite quotes. The idea is to subject yourself to something that empowers you to do your best, despite your circumstances.

Self-help reading need not always be boring. You can gain inspirational from the unlikeliest of places. For instance, a popular comic book or a fictional character you admire. Have fun in your pursuit of seeking motivation.

48. You are your loudest cheerleader. Even when you don't find others around you very encouraging or doubtful of your abilities, keep in mind that no one knows you like yourself and hence the person who is best suited to be your cheerleader is You. When you are preparing yourself for a challenging situation, indulge in a bit of self-pep talk. Tell yourself that no situation is bigger than your ability to tackle the situation or come out victorious. Express implicit confidence in your abilities through your words, thoughts, and actions.

Do not restrict yourself compliments only to seemingly big tasks and accomplishments. Pat yourself on the back for every little achievement, which in turn boosts your confidence and allows you to go after bigger goals. Tell yourself you have put your best foot forward even when you haven't performed according to your own expectations.

Acknowledge each time you managed to successfully achieve something; however small it seems. For instance, you submitted a project before the deadline or handled an irate customer maturely. These seemingly tiny things add up to our self-perception and invariably translate into greater positivity.

Another wonderful thing you can do is to reward yourself tangibly (with your favorite ice-cream or chocolate or book or coffee) for every accomplishment or achievement. This allows our self-approval thoughts to be directly linked to concrete benefits, which works wonders for our self-esteem and self-love.

49. Continue doing what you're a master at. There are some things that you do exceptionally well. Keep doing these things regularly to reinforce your faith in your remarkable strengths and talents. It can be anything from being an efficient administrator to being an excellent orator/communicator. Take on these tasks whenever you have the opportunity to do so. It

will not just make you feel productive, but also boost your self-esteem by several folds.

Increasing Self-esteem Through Writing and Journaling

You've heard about how some of the most powerful and successful people are into the habit of writing down their thoughts, feelings, actions, and goals. What is it about this practice that makes it so effective when it comes to being the person you want to be and living the life of your dreams? Why is writing down your goals and thoughts such a powerful self-transformation exercise? Here's everything you wanted to know about loving yourself and building higher confidence and self-esteem.

Maintaining a personal diary/journal has multiple positive benefits. Just like a hobby or therapy that allows us to vent out our pent-up feelings to achieve catharsis, journaling can be extremely therapeutic. Few things can track and enhance your personal development like journaling. Keeping a consistent record of your actions and self-affirmations allows you to obtain better insights about your goals and behavior.

Research has consistently pointed to the fact that maintaining a journal regularly can have a profound effect on your physical and psychological health. It can directly affect the way you feel about yourself and boost your self-esteem. It's proven to be highly effective for changing behavior patterns, overcoming addiction, problem-solving and goal setting. Journaling is also known to reduce stress and help you lead a more harmonious and fulfilled life. Here are some tips on practicing building higher self-esteem through journaling.

Keep a success log. Keep a section of your journal dedicated to all your success stories, however small they may seem to you. Once you get into the habit of chronicling your successes, you will gradually notice yourself feeling more and more confident. When you write, you are internalizing whatever you are written and sending out strong signals to your subconscious/unconscious mind, which in turn guides your mind to manifest more of those actions.

You can only work with your conscious mind; you really don't know what's stored in your subconscious or unconscious realm. However, internalizing by writing is a brilliant technique for accessing your subconscious and leveraging its power to direct the conscious mind into action. The more you write about how successfully you undertook a task, the more your subconscious will believe it to be true and guide your actions to be in sync with this belief, which will lead to more success stories.

Stay specific. If you're writing down your goals about what you want to achieve or how you aspire to be, be precise. Don't set vague goals that were written like you really don't know what exactly you want. Focus and be specific. If you want to be a highly confident person, don't just write that you want to be a more confident person.

What is it that you will do differently when you're a more confident person? How will you feel? How will walk and talk to people? How will people see you? Write everything that you expect to create when you're a more confident person. The more vividly you visualize and describe yourself after achieving your goal, the more likely you are to manifest it.

Specific details will also increase your accountability to your goals rather than simply stating them broadly and vaguely. You are less likely to abandon your goals when you state them explicitly.

Avoid being too logical. Don't be too focused on logic and keeping your goals seemingly realistic. What may seem highly unrealistic to you may be your reality tomorrow. Strange things happen. Life is full of surprises. You never know what you can manifest by tapping into your subconscious mind. Let your imagination run riot. Write about deepest desires and everything you want to achieve, even it if seems ridiculously optimistic.

Journaling is about writing your innermost thoughts and feelings, with little place for rational thinking. It is an intuitive exercise that seeks to connect to your deepest being. People are often scared of revealing their true desires, even to themselves. You may have imagined yourself on the stage giving a brilliant presentation to a packed house, followed by thundering applause.

However, in reality, you may see yourself as a socially awkward person who is barely able to strike a conversation, let alone speak in front of a crowd. While journaling, don't be afraid to record what you aspire to be, however impossible it seems. Write about how it feels to stand on that stage, how it feels to talk confidently in front of people and how you feel when people cheer you on. We are creating an alternative sphere of reality in our subconscious minds to ultimately direct our actions to be in tandem with these internalized feelings. Write as if you are experiencing it in the present.

Maintain a daily gratitude journal. Much as there are several things you would like to change about yourself, there are numerous others you are thankful for, isn't it? Life has given us all numerous gifts that we should be grateful for. A gratitude journal is nothing but a daily note about everything that happened in the day that we're thankful for.

It need not be big things. It can be all the wonderful gifts we enjoy such as nature, fresh air, electricity, water, shelter and more. This helps us thank a force (god, universe, guru or just about anyone/anything that we hold with reverence) for all the gifts we receive, and in turn, the positive energies help in creating more of what we are grateful for.

Focus on qualities that you admire about yourself. What are your strengths? Why are you grateful for them? How can you use them to make the world a better place to live? Your confidence and sense of self-worth will automatically increase when you start expressing gratitude for all the blessings in your life.

Write in the third person to get greater clarity. If you've been through a particularly challenging situation that has sent your self-esteem plunging down, gain a better perspective by writing in an objective, third-person voice for better clarity. Sometimes, we're so deeply involved and affected by things that happen to us that we fail to see them in the right perspective.

You were laid off from your job may have nothing to do with your skills or ability. It might be a simple business decision due to downsizing. Yet, this can be a huge blow to your confidence. You may stop believing in your ability to be a good worker.

However, writing about this situation from a third person perspective will allow you to view it with greater objectivity without taking it personally. This can help you shed your feelings of self-doubt and low self-confidence.

Make it personal and unique. Your journal should stand for everything you represent as a person, and aspire to be. It should be distinctly you. Decorate it with images that hold significance for you, draw caricatures, write chants, include quotes that motivate you, stick cartoons that inspire you- anything to make it unique and attractive.

You will be more comfortable pouring your heart out in a book if you're having fun doing it, and it inspires you to get back to it every day. If you're an artist, you can create images that come to your mind randomly. Often, this is a way through which our subconscious mind manifests itself. Be natural, spontaneous, unique and creative when it comes to creating your journal. You'll find it easier to connect to it.

Keep all affirmations ready. Another nice journaling tip for boosting your self-esteem is to keep all your affirmations handy. Devote a section to all the accolades and compliments you've won so far. It can be printouts of emails, appreciation letters from employers, Facebook messages, letters and anything else that sounds encouraging. It's a great way to uplift yourself when you're feeling a bit down. These affirmations turn out to be little blessings that reach out to you to let you know how fabulous you actually are. It encourages you to concentrate on your positives and build on it.

Pen your thoughts about someone you genuinely admire. If you want more motivation and inspiration, maintain a journal or a section of the journal for writing about a person who has always inspired you. It can be a teacher, a parent, your favorite sportsperson, an actor – anyone whose life journey and lessons have had a profound effect on you. Record things like what is it about them that really inspires you, what qualities of theirs would you like to imbibe, how you would feel if you reached where they are in life and other similar ideas. It will help you create more focused goals for yourself and boost your self-esteem.

Increasing Self-Esteem with Visualization

Visualization is often not as complicated as people make it out to be. In simple words, it is a process of using the power of mental imagery to help your brain develop greater confidence that can be manifested through actions. Research has pointed to the premise that your brain doesn't have the capacity to differentiate an imagined occurrence from an actual occurrence.

The brain's chemical reaction is the same for both. The brain invariably directs your actions to be in sync with these feelings – whether real or imaginary. Thus, helping you actually, create everything you've seen through your mind's eye. When you keep thinking about the positive outcome of a highly anticipated event, don't you experience a noticeably feel good syndrome? This, in turn, helps you create a positive outcome with the help of actions directed by your subconscious mind.

Be as descriptive as possible. If you want to gain more confidence or enhance your self-esteem, visualize yourself as a highly confident person. Create mental scenarios of how you will come across when you're more confident and self-assured. Be as descriptive as possible. What are you wearing? How are you behaving? What are you talking? How do you feel?

Act like it is happening in the present and not something that's slated to happen in the future. How does it feel to be a more confident and self-loving person? You are doing nothing but internalizing the qualities of a confident person. This is the first step to being the confident person you aspire to be.

Concentrate on specifics. People who complain about the inefficiency of the visualization technique are often those who do not focus on the specifics or have slimly targeted goals. Visualization works brilliantly if you have laser targeted goals and know exactly what you want.

Imagine a scenario where you aspire for more confidence when it comes to public speaking. You want to be an ace at presentations and win thundering applause. Now, while practicing visualization, simply close your eyes and see yourself talking confidently on the stage. Be specific about the details. How does the set-up look? What kind of people are a part of the audience? What are you talking about? How do your voice sound and feel? How's the sound of the applause? Do you get it? Don't be vague. The more specific you are about details, the easier it is to embed these details into your mind and transform them into reality.

Avoid being bogged down by reality. Thinking about what's possible and not possible is not your job. Your job is to imagine and visualize. Don't be held down by thoughts of, "Oh! This is so impossible; it's never going to happen in this lifetime." You might be in for a huge surprise.

Don't underestimate the power of your subconscious mind. Don't be too concerned about having seemingly unrealistic goals. Think and visualize big. Even if you break into cold sweat talking to a group of four, visualize yourself addressing a huge crowd.

Visualization is not about logic or reality. It is about achieving your fullest potential, which unfortunately even you may not be aware of. Sometimes, due to our inability to believe in ourselves or negative experiences in life, we tend to undermine our true potential. Our visualization exercises shouldn't reflect what we believe we can do, but what we want to do. They are meant to fun, creative and enjoyable mindful exercises that allow our imagination to run wild.

Visualize or think of someone confident. Visualize a person you believe is really confident. Imagine how he/she walks, talks carries himself/herself and greets people. What you are really doing is internalizing their qualities and training your physical self into acting in a similar manner. Make a conscious effort to analyze your actions mentally. Assess your body language and how to conduct yourself around people the next time you are with a group.

Make a mental note of your tone, gestures, posture, and expressions. Make your visualization thoughts powerful and vivid. You will eventually find yourself emulating the person you've been imagining because the mind will send strong signals to your body to act in coordination with these thoughts.

Practice guided meditation. You can combine principles of guided meditation with journaling to create a comprehensive visualization technique. Guided meditation is nothing but a step by step instructional narrative by which the practitioner is mentally taken through a scenario, while he/she is meditating. It can be conducted by a trained instructor or even a recording.

The idea is to gradually go with the flow until you can completely immerse yourself in a specific scenario. This can be followed by journaling your experience at the end of the session about your thoughts, feelings and physical reactions while living the scene mentally. The key is to get you to live the experience as if it is actually happening or you are actually living it.

Repetition is the key. Have you ever heard powerful orators speak? Why do they keep saying the same things several times during their speech? What's the point of repeating something they've already communicated? The principle behind it is to repeat it as many times as possible to drill the idea into your psyche.

It's the same with visualization exercises. The more repetitively you imagine something, the more you're drilling it into your subconscious to create it. Repeating self-affirmations, visualizations and journal writings is a great way to get your mind to act of these affirmations.

Thus, you can imagine yourself as a self-assured and confident individual, while saying, "I am a confident and self-assured person who loves interacting with people" several times during the day.

Not done with self-esteem yet? Here are some more productive and powerful tips for boosting your self-esteem like never before.

Grow a Like-Minded Network or Community

As you embark on the journey of following your passion, you encounter several passionate, enthusiastic and like-minded people who share your goals. They become part of a strong support community and connections, who help you gain back your lost confidence. They come up with fresh ideas to expand your horizon, boost your options and enhance creativity.

This not just helps in creating a more rewarding life for yourself but also helps you transform into a more self-assured, evolved and aware individual.

Participate Actively in a Cause You Strongly Believe In

Few things make you feel as good about yourself as when you make a difference to other lives. When you contribute meaningfully to add value to those less fortunate than you, you create a powerful circle of love. Support a cause you are passionate about. Be involved in it by actively making time for it, contributing ideas and making life easier for others. Nothing is as gratifying as utilizing your expertise for helping people.

When you are deeply involved in giving, you feel wonderful about yourself, and your spirit is instantly uplifted. You also experience greater gratitude for the gifts you have when you closely experience the life of those less fortunate than you. This makes you feel more appreciative and thankful for everything you are, which in turn boosts self-esteem.

Build Self-Esteem with Your Passion and Productivity

Are you completely in love with your life? Are you taking up pursuits that excite you? Are you chasing activities you are passionate about such as traveling around the world, playing a sport or doing volunteer work? A majority of the folks aren't living a life of their dreams by pursuing their passion. They are living a life of desperation and compulsion dictated by the practical necessities. Life is all about following a routine and creating status quos. Displaying the confidence and courage to run after your passion allows you to lead a more fulfilling life, which results in greater self-love.

Test Yourself

When was the last time you challenged yourself by moving out of your comfort zone? When was the last time you did something you were afraid of doing earlier? When was the last time you achieved something that you'd never thought you could achieve?

Chasing your passion allows you to challenge yourself. It allows you to unlock the potential which you may or may not be aware of. When you take on something that you had always wanted to do but were unsure of doing, you are taking your fears head-on. You are proving to yourself you have unlimited reserves of courage to face and overcome your looming fears. This can be the ultimate emotions and self-esteem booster.

Challenging yourself to push your boundaries by following your passion can help you explore your true potential and virtues.

Follow Tiny Pursuits

When it comes to following your passion, everything need not be about life-altering decisions. You can practice this in the smallest of ways by doing things you've always wanted to do. For instance, you may have wanted to learn a foreign language or belly dancing or become a trained singer or a master of Italian cuisine. We all have those passions we wish we had pursued earlier. It is never too late. Make time for these activities in your life to experience a new surge of positivity.

When you master things you've always wanted to learn, you feel a great sense of pride and accomplishment, which can work wonders for your self-esteem and self-love.

Realign Your Notion of Failure

The biggest reason people are afraid of pursuing their passion can be pinned down to their fear of failure. One of the best ways to love yourself again is to take up something you've always wanted to do or passions you've wanted to pursue without being held back by the fear of failure.

Reframing your concept of failure as defined by the world will allow you to lead a more content and fulfilling life. If you understand the concept of failure is subjective, you may be able to chase things that light your fire. For some, success may mean more money. For you, it may mean more enriching experiences.

So, for someone else, you may be a failure if you take up volunteer assignments across the globe or teach English to children in underdeveloped nations. However, for you, it may be a successful and gratifying feeling like no other. Reframing your concept of failure is important when it comes to pursuing your passion and increasing your self-esteem.

Uncertainties and Risks Help You Grow

The path to exploring your passion can be filled with risks and uncertainties. It is stepping into an unknown zone and living without knowing the outcome of your decision. However, without taking calculated and well-planned risks we may not experience much growth or expand the horizon of opportunities. Getting comfortable with risks and uncertainty is the highway to discovering our true potential and bringing ourselves back on the path of self-love.

Develop Higher Self-Awareness

When you explore and chase your passion, you learn a great deal about yourself. You realize what you are exceptionally good at and what your deepest desires are. You get a true glimpse of your personality, aptitude, intelligence, and skills. This leads to greater healing and a sense of enlightenment. When you know your innermost self, you find it easy to celebrate your positives and accept the negatives. Self-awareness increases your ability to love yourself unconditionally.

Habits That Destroy Your Self-Esteem, Emotions, and Positivity

Habits that you engage in, often mindlessly, can define you. It can be anything that seems harmless to you like leaving your work desk cluttered or being on your phone while eating breakfast. What makes habits so powerful is they are carried out without much mindfulness yet have a huge impact on us.

Habits are more a product of our subconscious/unconscious mind, which have evolved over the years. Therefore, we don't give much thought to them and also carry them out more as reflex actions. However, being more mindful of your everyday habits can boost your self-esteem/self-confidence in greater ways than you can realize. Habits determine our actions, which in turn can deeply influence our self-esteem. Here are some habits that may unknowingly be gnawing on your sense of self-worth.

1. Investing a majority of your time on wasteful sedentary activities - You aren't going to feel too good about yourself and your body while sitting on the couch the entire day. Physical activities can help you feel wonderful about yourself and keep you in top health. Sweating it out, being fit and staying healthy makes you more confident about yourself, enhances your mood and reduces social withdrawal symptoms.

When you devote time to fitness and your body, you start leading a fitter and more balanced lifestyle, which increases your self-esteem. On the other hand, being unfit and unhealthy by indulging only in sedentary activities can decrease your self-confidence, and make you more prone to feelings of depression and loneliness.

2. Perpetual comparisons with others - While healthy competition can be good, unhealthy comparisons aren't. All of us invariably fall into the trap of evaluating ourselves and our lives in comparison with others, which ends up making us feel lesser than others. What happens when you realize you have performed much better than you did previously? You feel positive, encouraged and motivated to do even better. Then, you notice that your peers have performed better than you have, and all the confidence and positivity nosedives. Focus on your performance, goals, and efforts. Understand that as long as you're improving your performance, it doesn't matter how you fare vis-à-vis others.

3. Unmanageable clutter - Uncontrollable clutter can make your life chaotic in more ways than you actually think possible. You accumulate a lot of things in the home and office and then just leave it there in a disorganized pile of mess. It saps your energy to find things. It makes you late because you've spent more time looking for things that you should have.

This habit reinforces your lack of organization, shoddy time management, and acute procrastination. Imagine you're preparing for a huge presentation and you're unable to locate your folder in the clutter. You're nervous as hell. You've ruined the intention. You feel low on confidence as you walk in to give your presentation and people notice it. It's a cycle.

Lack of planning and organization skills can deeply impact your self-esteem. It takes little time and effort to get organized, but the efforts are worth it. Plan ahead, organize your desk neatly, categorize your folders for easy access, and get rid of unwanted clutter. You will see the huge difference these small changes make in your life.

4. Being a people pleaser - It's not going to happen. Don't aim to please everyone every time. People pleasers are not just soft targets for bullies, but also unproductive and non-assertive. They tend to let people take advantage of them and ruin their self-esteem. Self-loving folks will always stand up for themselves in an assertive manner and refuse to do what they don't think they should.

It saves them time, effort, energy, and helps them utilize these elements for more productive tasks. Learn to distinguish between genuine people and tasks, and those that simply sap your energy for their benefit. Saying "no" when you don't want to or can't do something in a polite, yet self-assured manner is absolutely alright.

5. Spending a lot of time on the internet - While the whole world is on the Internet, devoting an unreasonably high time for online activities can hit your self-esteem like few other things. You often find yourself comparing yourself/your life to what others portray about their life (which may or may not be true) on social media. There is an excessive tendency to be what you aren't, to live a life that may currently be beyond your means, and a general feeling of hopelessness, which leads to diminished confidence.

Instead, focus on your life, and keep in mind that newsfeeds are nothing but selective bits of information where people put across the best versions of their life. Get active in real life rather than surfing the Net for hours on end. Meet new people. Join hobby clubs. Play a sport. Try and attend more parties to socialize with real people. When you talk to new people, make new acquaintances and increase your friend's circle, it will reflect on the way you feel about yourself.

6. **Avoid playing the victim** - Avoid getting into a reactive mindset and playing victim all the time. Don't act like you are being a victim of circumstances that are beyond your control every time. Playing victim strips us of the power within us. We get into a mindset of helplessness, which isn't often true. We can only feel strong, worthy and confident when shaking off the victim mindset and take charge of our life. When we take onus for our actions and reactions, we empower ourselves to change our circumstances proactively, rather than playing reactive victims. This automatically increases our self-esteem.

7. **Do not procrastinate** - Yes, some people get a sort of adrenaline rush while performing their tasks at the far end of the deadline. We feel we thrive in stressful situations. However, this is just another fancy cover-up for our lack of organization

and planning skills. We wait until the last minute to submit an assignment, pay our bills, refill gas or repair a plumbing fault. Our minds naturally avoid doing things at the moment and put them off for later.

This increases stress, anxiety and can result in inconvenience or poor performance. We do things in a hurry to finish them at the last moment and end up doing them badly, which invariably affects our confidence. Practice being fully mindful of unrequired stress that drains our energy and confidence.

Seek to break these habits by making small and practiced changes in your life. Get out of this unhealthy pattern by diverting your energy into more positive actions that reduce stress, improve your performance and help you lead a more hassle-free life.

8. No substance abuse - This should be a no-brainer. People who rely on substances such as drugs, nicotine, alcohol, and caffeine to help them cope with everyday challenges definitely lack the confidence to face these issues. Abusing substances or engaging in addictive behavior is a sure-shot sign of ignoring the root of your problem. It seems like a lucrative quick-fix, but you aren't tackling the deeper issue.

Addictions lower your morale when you are unable to get "your fix" and find it challenging to cope with the situation without it. There is excessive reliance on a force outside you and not within you, which can be hugely de-motivating. You are being controlled by destructive elements rather than being in control.

9. Avoid putting off people - Do you find yourself putting off replying to an email to a long-lost friend or the voicemail you received from your parents? Do you have trouble returning people's calls? The more you put off contacting people who're genuinely concerned about you or may have some important information for you, the more it feels like a stressful burden that exhausts you.

10. Treating people badly - It is often said that how we treat others is a reflection of how we feel about ourselves. The more we respect and treat others well, the more we get closer to loving and respecting ourselves. Treat others as you would want them to treat you. Don't always treat people in a condescending manner or humiliate them or hurt their self-esteem. Rather, focus on building it with positive talk and motivation. Instead of focusing on how badly they did something, concentrate on what they did well and how they can improve. You will notice the powerful change this will have on your own self-esteem.

Chapter 6:
Emotions and Our Immediate Environment – Clear the Clutter

Cleaning your room or closet can be more rewarding than you believe. It not just helps your de-clutter the old and make way for new, but is also therapeutic when it comes to cleansing your mind. An organized space often reflects an organized and chaos-free mind, which paves the path of self-acceptance, self-love and greater ability to manage our emotions.

Even a simple act of taking time out to clean your cupboard will have a positive effect on your state of being. Getting rid of old and unwanted clutter that consumes energy allows you to make space for the refreshing new things that await you in life.

Releases the Feeling of Being Emotionally Stagnant

Keeping gifts from past lovers or friends where relationships have gone sour haunts you and make you latch on to an unpleasant past that may have devastated your self-esteem.

Getting rid of these objects releases you from getting stuck in an unfortunate past and makes you look forward to the future.

There may be certain things or objects that remind you of specific negative periods in your life. Clearing out the clutter will give you an opportunity to release painful memories or feelings attached to these objects. You really do not want to keep anything that brings a negative vibration. Do not keep things that are a reminder of what has already happened.

Creativity Thrives in a Clutter-Free Atmosphere

When you free yourself from the shackles of unwanted stuff, you are more open to positive energy or a lifeforce. Creativity is manifested through positive life energy when it operates without any obstruction.

Whenever we can't create anything or there is a barrier to our creative energy, we use the term "blocked," for instance, writer's block. Clutter clearance gets our energy unblocked once again to allow creativity to flourish. When you are creative and productive, your sense of self-worth and ability to control emotions dramatically improve.

Your Immediate Environment is a Direct Reflection of Your Inner State

The space we live in is a reflection of our inner state. The more present, balanced and still your life is, the less inclined you will be to live in the midst of chaos. Things may or may not be in your control, but you can control how you feel by choosing to live in an organized and non-messy space. Even if you aren't in a very good place in your life currently, you can quickly change the way you feel by cleaning up and staying organized.

Opportunities Open Up

How many times has it happened that you've come across that lost business proposal email while clearing your mailbox or the contact details of a long-lost associate who can be of help to you currently? Or found money tucked somewhere where you'd totally forgotten you'd left it? Money and opportunity are the most positive effects of de-cluttering. You open up yourself to greater positivity, money, and opportunity in the process of clearing your space.

Higher Mental Focus

Clear spaces give you the ability to think, curate, organize and process information more sharply. It enhances your concentration and mental focus. When you can think more clearly and focus, you automatically accomplish greater results, which lead to a higher sense of self-esteem. A clogged space, on the other hand, saps up your ability to focus on a single thing and diverts your energies in multiple, unwanted directions.

Reduces Anxiety

Clutter is often a sign of unfinished, unattended and neglected tasks. It is junk that we haven't bothered to finish or confront. They pile up and loom into our immediate surroundings that lead to anxious thoughts and actions. Anxiousness associated with unfinished tasks or bad memories is not conducive for self-esteem or emotional intelligence. Dealing with your pent-up chores in a mindful and conscious manner elevates feelings of nervousness and anxiety to make you a more confident individual.

Start Small

Begin with a small routine and commit to keeping at it, while gradually raising the de-cluttering bar for yourself. Start by committing to doing the dishes twice a day and throwing the thrash. Even these small acts of tending to routine household chores can reduce anxiety and make life seem less overwhelming. When you complete daily chores, it gives you a wonderful sense of accomplishment, which can be a huge boost for your self-esteem and self-confidence.

Increase Productivity

It is not rocket science. When the clutter within your space is cleared, you don't have many physical obstacles that prevent you from being more productive and efficient. You can achieve so much more in comparatively lesser time when you don't have to work in a disorganized set-up. Imagine spending half an hour only to locate a project file that you have to work on in a pile of files and unfinished tasks. Then submitting the project late because it took you another half an hour to locate the research papers.

Your boss is fuming and doesn't spare any words to tell you how disorganized and behind the time you are. What does this do to your self-esteem? When you live and work in a clutter-free set-up, you pave the way for greater productivity by operating more efficiently. This can-do wonders for your self-esteem because it lifts your confidence and makes you view yourself in a positive light.

Allow the New to Come In

Letting go of the old allows you to make room for the new. When you cleanse your space, you are actually cleansing your soul to release yourself from painful memories, negative thoughts or unwanted baggage from the past. When you are free from the negativity of the past, it is easier to embrace the positivity of the future. Shedding the old allows you to make room for the new. Get rid of the negative space in your home and mind and replace it with more positive thoughts and feelings, thus boosting self-love.

Chapter 7:
Explore Your Spiritual Side for Managing Anger and Other Destructive Emotions

Faith is the bedrock for increasing your self-esteem and emotional intelligence. It makes you believe, irrespective of the prevailing circumstances and situation. Firmly believing in a higher power allows your soul to be open to the wonders of faith, hope, and trust. Spirituality helps in building your intuition and getting you closer to your inner voice. It helps you make sound decisions based on a powerful gut feeling.

Your spiritual quest can help you discover new things about yourself. It can lead to new thoughts, beliefs, passions, emotions, feelings, and actions. You will come to appreciate yourself more when you are able to establish a stronger connection with your inner self, which in turn will assist you in managing your emotions even more effectively.

Managing your emotions and self-healing can be practiced in several effective ways including mindfulness and meditation. One of the most fundamental lessons of spiritualism is loving and accepting ourselves unconditionally. You are part of the entire universe and it is as important to love yourself as it is to love others. When dealing with destructive emotions, one of the best ways is to take control back from the emotion into your hands.

Meditation and mindfulness will allow you to dictate how you should express your anger rather than the emotions dictating your actions. Practicing self-love and learning to manage your emotions is the key to dealing with potentially damaging emotions.

Self-esteem and managing emotions are predominantly about unconditional acceptance of oneself, with compassion, understanding and appreciation sprinkled in. Can you wholeheartedly accept yourself the way you are currently? If no, what is it that you seek to completely accept yourself? Do you want to be more successful? Or look better? Or perhaps enhance your communication skills? We attach several conditions to our list of "the ideal me."

Do you have it in you to love yourself without fulfilling specific self-conditions or do you have to live up to personal expectations to gain acceptance from yourself? Will you love yourself even if you do not become what you wanted to become? When you practice self-love, there is lesser anger, resentment, frustration and negativity within you.

The gifts of developing a higher sense of self-worth are plentiful from the perspective of developing healthier emotions and glowing self-esteem. Those with a healthy and balanced idea of self-esteem are also able to love and accept others more effortlessly. When you practice greater self-love, you are actually telling yourself and the universe that you deserve all the great things in life. This gradually allows your hopes, dreams, and desires to manifest into your reality for leading a more fulfilling life, which in turn helps keep your negative emotions in check. Here are some powerful tips to help you discover your spirituality for managing negative emotions.

Interpreting Dreams

Spiritual healing or cleansing can be highly effective when it comes to increasing your self-esteem. It can be practiced in multiple ways such as self-hypnosis, dream interpretation, yoga, reiki, aromatherapy, qigong and much more.

Dream interpretation is a fantastic way to tune into your inner self. Our dreams hold the key to facets of our mind which remain locked – the subconscious and unconscious mind. Increasing awareness about our dreams and interpreting them accurately helps us dive into our subconscious and establish a more powerful connection with self. What is it that is holding us back? What are the overpowering emotions that are preventing us from leading a more balanced life? What are the feelings that we need to get rid of to love ourselves again? What is stopping us from achieving what we want in life? What are our positives which can be used to fulfill these goals?

The roadway to self-healing and self-acceptance becomes simpler when we are aware of our innermost feelings. The universe and our mind are always trying to communicate with us through metaphors and symbols in our dreams. Unlocking these dreams gives us the power to accept, appreciate and love ourselves even more. Connecting with the higher mind allows us to live a more rewarding, meaningful and fulfilling life.

Convincing the Sub Conscious with Affirmations

Think of your subconscious mind as a computer that holds vital information. If you have to change the information (read beliefs held in our subconscious), you have to reprogram the machine.

Repeating an affirmation every day allows you to "reprogram your subconscious" and direct it towards believing more positive things about yourself. The practice channelizes your subconscious to love yourself unconditionally. Affirmations can be spoken, written (more on journaling later) or repeated in the mind.

Identify Your Positive Space

All of us have that one place which instantly transforms the way we are feeling. It can be your local library or a city park or even your garage. This is the place that helps you channelize your positive energies with intention and serenity. If you don't already have a happy place, go and find it. It can also be a quiet corner in your house where you feel completely at peace with yourself. Notice the quick change in your emotional frequency when you visit your 'positive space.'

Your happy place helps you connect with yourself in an inspiring environment. It allows you to free yourself from thoughts related to everyday life to focus on your inner self. You can do everything from having conversations with yourself to writing down your most profound thoughts here. Experience the inspiring energy of the place.

Meditate

Meditation allows you to view yourself in a calmer and non-judgmental state of mind. In simple terms, it allows you to get introduced to and strike a meaningful friendship with yourself. You gain a better awareness of who you are and learn to embrace and accept every aspect of your being. Any doubts, fears, suspicions, and insecurities with automatically vanish when you get to know who you really are. These superficial feelings will have no place when you establish a deeper connection of trust and dignity with yourself.

As you gradually begin to accept yourself with kindness and understanding, you slay self-destructive clauses held inside you that you are not good enough or you do not deserve life's good things or you don't deserve to be happy. Basically, you invite more compassion into the cycle of self-negation and low self-worth, until the uncertainty or negative feelings are completely dissolved in the powerful feeling of self-love.

Find a serene, relaxing and comfortable place to practice self-loving meditation. Practice deep breathing. Take a few conscious and deep breaths. Focus on the flow of the breath as you breathe in and breathe out. Be aware of your body parts as you practice mindful breathing and meditation. Start with the heart, and feel the heart softening, beating and opening up as you breathe.

Now, visualize yourself in your heart. You can imagine a picture of yourself inside your heart or chant your name multiple times. Keep holding yourself within your heart lovingly and gently. Repeat an affirmation that focuses on freeing you from self-doubt, being happy and living positively. "May I be happy forever" or "May I break away from the cycle of self-doubt." Holding yourself tenderly and repeating the affirmation will slowly help you develop a more compassionate, deeper and appreciative relationship with yourself. Finally, take a deep breath and let all negativity in the form of pent up stress, tension or resistance release.

Another way is to imagine your persona as that of being your child. Think of yourself as the parent and your personality as your own child. Imagine this child to be a perfect creation. It is still growing and developing to reach its potential, but it is perfect at its current stage. Accept your child whole-heartedly, just the way it is. Look at the miracle of nature with fondness, appreciation, and kindness, with all its positives and negatives. Open your heart to this child completely and embrace it with unconditional love.

Exercise

Exercise is as much a spiritually fulfilling and cleansing process as it is a physically rewarding activity. When you show greater love and respect for your body, you invariably show greater love for yourself. Participating in exciting and challenging pursuits allows nourishment of your spirit, which in turn makes you feel better about yourself once again.

Have you ever experienced the immediate shift in your state of mind when you run or undertake a physically challenging activity after feeling low? Don't you feel all charged up and raring to go? This is what intense activity can do to your spirit. It helps you shed the negative feelings and focus on the positivity of your body to pave the way for greater self-love.

Deepen Awareness

Deepening your awareness is practicing genuine soul-searching. It is knowing where you are currently placed where self-love is concerned. Is there a deficit of self-love? What are the underlying issues which have led to this shortage? Quiet reflection is a great way to bring light into your unconscious mind to identify deeper issues.

Ask yourself questions that help you talk to your inner self. What is it that you love about yourself? What is it that is preventing you from having a glowing opinion about yourself? What would you like to change about yourself? It is like connecting with your "mental therapist" to figure out how you can practice greater self-love or build your self-esteem. Yes, your inner self can be your best therapist. No one knows you like your deep, inner self, and tapping into it is akin is talking to a close pal about your deepest, most heartfelt feelings.

You are simply doing an unbiased and critical analysis of yourself. There is no scope for right or wrong or judging your actions. It is taking stock on what's functionally wonderfully and what you can work on to make yourself even more fabulous than you already are. This will help you fine-tune aspects of your personality that you want to change.

Allow Intuition to Lead You

You open yourself up for greater self-love when you learn to be guided by your intuition. When we listen to and act on our inner voice, it helps us establish a better connection with our internal forces. Look for clues and signs that instantly give you a powerful gut feeling. When something feels right or wrong, it probably is just that. Make an effort to build your intuition by meditating or having conversations with yourself.

When you learn to communicate with your inner voice, you find it easier to make seek guidance and make decisions. This will allow you to experience greater self-love. Your decisions will seem less mechanical and more driven by an inner voice, which will offer you a deeper sense of joy, gratification, and fulfillment.

Make Gratitude a Habit

Make a conscious effort to let go of toxic comparisons and be thankful for what the gifts you possess. Leading a life of gratitude will allow you to love and accept yourself while letting go of harsh judgments, bitter frustrations and a feeling of hopelessness. The negative feelings will be replaced by greater possibilities and avenues for happiness.

Gratitude can be practiced by affirming your thankfulness for everything you have, writing a list of things you are thankful to the universe for and thanking others more often for the smallest things. When your heart is in a state of peace and thankfulness, it is easier to love and accept yourself for who you are.

Nobody can be you as good as you. Being thankful for the gifts you have, however small they may seem, manifests even more of these gifts.

Prayers

Prayers can be extremely healing and cleansing when it comes to having faith in yourself, accepting yourself and increasing your self-esteem. Irrespective of your spiritual or religious beliefs, prayers can be great stress relievers and miracle enforcers. They can boost your faith and belief, which in turn can make you more self-assured and self-loving.

Being a part of healing circles can also make you feel wonderful about yourself. If you want to experience the collective power of prayers and positive energy, participate in local healing circles that make you feel supported and cared for. The positivity of other people who believe in the power of faith and prayers can transform the way you think about yourself. This, in turn, has a direct bearing on your feelings and emotions.

Conclusion

Thank you for downloading this book.

I hope you enjoyed reading it and were able to learn the finer aspects of managing your emotions and developing a higher sense of self-esteem. I also hope it offered you plenty of actionable strategies, practical tips, and wisdom gems to transform negative emotions into positive ones to lead a more fulfilling life.

The best part is unlike conventional intelligence, emotional intelligence can be developed through regular practice, training, and application. Improving your emotional awareness and ability to manage emotions is a continuous and dynamic process that only helps you lead a more well-rounded personal and professional life.

The next step is to simply go out there and use all the proven strategies mentioned in the book. You can't become an expert at managing emotions overnight simply by reading about it. Apply the strategies mentioned in the book in your daily life to witness awesome results!

You'll gradually transform from someone who struggles with their emotions to an emotionally evolved and socially adept individual, who will enjoy better interpersonal relationships and professional success in life.

If you enjoyed reading the book, I would recommend another manuscript called "Social Skills Guidebook", is a practical guide to overcome shyness towards others and learn to relate perfectly with the rest of the world. Finally, please take time out to share your feedback by posting a review. It'd be highly appreciated

Printed in Great Britain
by Amazon